A LITTLE GIANT® BOOK

WHODUNIT MYSTERIES

Jim Sukach, Hy Conrad, Stan Smith,
Derrick Niederman, Tom Bullimore, Falcon Travis

Illustrated by Lucy Corvino, Ian Anderson, Kathleen
O'Malley, Matt LeFleur

STERLING

New York / London
www.sterlingpublishing.com/kids

Published by Sterling Publishing Co., Inc.
387 Park Avenue South, New York, NY 10016

10 9 8 7 6 5 4 3 2

Distributed in Canada by Sterling Publishing
c/o Canadian Manda Group, 165 Dufferin Street
Toronto, Ontario, Canada M6K 3H6
Distributed in the United Kingdom by GMC Distribution Services,
Castle Place, 166 High Street, Lewes, East Sussex, England BN7 1XU
Distributed in Australia by Capricorn Link (Australia) Pty. Ltd.
P.O. Box 704, Windsor, NSW 2756, Australia

Printed in China

Sterling ISBN-13: 978-1-4027-4983-4
       ISBN-10: 1-4027-4983-X

For information about custom editions, special sales, premium and
corporate purchases, please contact Sterling Special Sales
Department at 800-805-5489 or specialsales@sterlingpub.com.

Contents

INSPECTOR WILL KETCHUM

The Sneak Thief

INSPECTOR WILL KETCHUM was off duty. He had just arrived at the train station to meet some friends, but their train was running an hour late. As he strolled across the main terminal, a man with the restless eyes of a sneak thief attracted his attention. Then he was lost in a sudden surge of passengers.

A few minutes later, the Inspector spotted the man, who was entering the station's coffee shop. Now he was carrying a leather briefcase.

The man sat at a vacant corner table, placing the briefcase between his chair and the wall.

The Inspector casually followed him in, sat at his table and, identifying himself as a police officer, asked if the man would mind stepping over to the Station Master's office to answer a few questions about the ownership of the briefcase that he had with him. The man claimed indignantly that the briefcase was his, but he agreed to go along.

In the Station Master's office the briefcase lay open on the desk, revealing a file of papers and an envelope containing about $200 in twenty-dollar bills.

"Before we opened the briefcase, Mr. Fink," began the Inspector, "you told us it was definitely yours and that it contained only a couple of magazines. Now you deny that you are the owner. How do you explain that?"

Mr. Fink rubbed his chin and looked puzzled. "This definitely isn't the briefcase I handed in at the checkroom this morning," he said.

"They must have given me someone else's. It looks exactly like mine, but I can see it isn't, now that it's open. My briefcase was locked and all it had in it were some magazines I was reading on the train. The owner of this briefcase shouldn't have left it unlocked with all this money in it. If he got mine by mistake, he isn't going to be very happy about it."

"I'm sure he won't be," said the Inspector. "What's more, he's probably wondering, as I am, why anyone would check a briefcase that had only a couple of magazines in it."

"That's easy to explain," said Mr. Fink. "I got to town this morning just before noon on one of those one-day round-trip excursion tickets—and I'll be going back tonight—if you don't make me miss my train. I was reading the magazines on the train. I brought my briefcase because I was hoping to find some second-hand books, but I didn't get to the bookstores because I met an old friend who invited me over to his house."

"So that's when you checked your briefcase?"

"That's right," continued Mr. Fink. "I didn't want to carry it around with me, so I left it here

and went to visit with my friend. Got my taxi fare paid both ways, had a great time, and all I had to spend since I got off the train this morning was what they charged me at the checkroom."

"Lucky you," said the Inspector. "Now, would you mind emptying out all your pockets and placing their contents on this desk?"

"I don't mind at all," said Mr. Fink. "I've got nothing to hide. The sooner you're satisfied, the sooner I can get going. I have to take this brief-case back to the checkroom and see if mine is still there."

Mr. Fink's statement and the contents of his pockets (on page 10) were enough to tell Will Ketchum whether or not the suspect was telling the truth.

What do you think?

Solution on page 313.

The Crypto Caper

SERGEANT ZUPP came into Inspector Ketchum's office and handed him a sheet of paper.

"We took this from one of the members of Crypto," said the Sergeant. "We have him in the next room. His boss likes using secret codes. It's too soon to make any sense out of it, but it doesn't look like it's going to be too much of a problem. Only eight letters of the alphabet seem to be in code; the rest are left unchanged. Instead of the eight letters, they've used eight figures from 2 to 9. I suppose they didn't use the figures 1 and 0 because they didn't want them to get mixed up with the letters I and O."

"Strictly speaking," said Will Ketchum, "this is a cipher. That short code-breaking course we had to take—because of Crypto's activities—has helped us to put most of them behind bars."

He took a scrap of paper, copied out the

message, and handed the original back to the Sergeant. "Return this to the suspect," he said, "looking as puzzled as you can, and let him go.

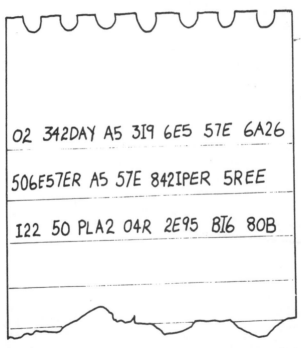

O2 342DAY A5 3I9 6E5 57E 6A26

506E57ER A5 57E 842IPER 5REE

I22 50 PLA2 O4R 2E95 BI6 80B

His boss still thinks we're too dumb to break his codes. This one won't take long."

Can you decipher the message?

Solution on page 313.

Crypto Strikes Again

"**WHAT DO YOU MAKE OF THIS, INSPECTOR?**" asked Detective DiAnsa. She handed him a folded sheet of paper. "I was questioning a suspect about a stolen car that he said he had just bought secondhand. This fell out of his wallet while he was looking for the receipt."

"A receipt he couldn't find?" said Inspector Will Ketchum.

The detective nodded.

The Inspector examined the sheet of paper. "This is almost certainly a Crypto communication. It could be important. So could your suspect. The brains behind the organization doesn't trust telephones, so the top boys pass coded messages when they're planning something big. Where is the suspect and what did he have to say about this?"

"He's in the station house," said Donna

DiAnsa. "He says he must have picked up the piece of paper at home, by mistake. It belongs to his son, who's a Boy Scout."

```
% = ? $ @   ? & $   ₣ * " $ + :
A F T E R   T H E         L T O

₮ % @ % ₮ $   ( $ ₣ $ " $ @ ₮
P A R A D E   E   E     E R

! & + ₮   ( + -   ? & $   ! & % @ $
h   ₴             T H E     h A R E

+ ₴ ?   ₣ * " "   - $   % ?   ? & $
    T       E   A T   T h E

= * ) $   ( + " " ₮   ! % * " + @ !
F     E               A       R

? % ) $ @ :   ? $ " "   : ₴ ? ? ₮
T A   E R     T E L L       T T

% : ₮ % " |   ? +   - $   ? & $ @ $
A     A L   T O     E   T h E R E
```

"Get me a copy of it," said the Inspector. "Then give it back to him with our compliments. This code is made up of typewriter symbols. And by the look of it, your man has already begun to decode it. You must have interrupted him. He only got as far as the first word and filled in the same letters throughout the message."

When Donna DiAnsa got Inspector Ketchum a copy of the message, he went to work on it. Detective DiAnsa kept the suspect talking until Ketchum was finished. Then the man was allowed to leave, but he was followed.

What did the message say?

Solution on page 314.

The Holdup

INSPECTOR KETCHUM was just passing Jackson's Stationery Shop when he heard on his cell phone that the manager, Mr. Prince, had been held up at knifepoint and robbed of the week's receipts.

The Inspector went inside and interviewed Mr. Prince.

"It happened while my new assistant Roger was out delivering a package. A man in a blue raincoat came into the shop and asked for a cheap ballpoint pen. He handed me a five-dollar bill and when I opened the cash drawer to give him his change, he pulled a knife and ordered me to put all the cash into a plastic bag he took from his pocket.

"He got all the bills and most of the change when my assistant Roger came in the front door. The man pushed past me and ran

through the stockroom and out the back door.
I'd say he was left-handed. He dropped the knife on his way out, and I left it where it fell in

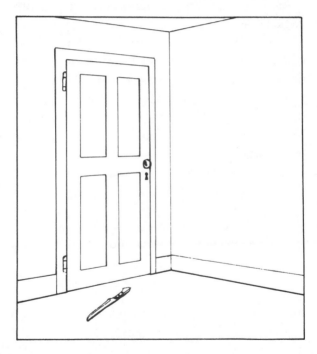

case it has fingerprints on it. I saw the man before he came into the shop. He was across the street talking to Roger."

Said Roger, "When I went out to deliver the package, a man in a blue raincoat stopped me and asked the way to Southport. I told him where to get the bus and he went off in that direction. When I got back, I heard shouting as I opened the door and saw Mr. Prince run into the stockroom. I didn't see anybody else, only Mr. Prince. Then he phoned the police and our home office."

Inspector Ketchum considered the two statements, took a look at the weapon, and made an arrest.

Whom did he arrest and why?

Solution on page 314.

Murder in the Locked Room

INSPECTOR WILL KETCHUM was called to Waverly Mansion to help local police with their investigation into the death of Dudley Pinlever, the famous philanthropist. He had been found shot dead, slumped over his desk in the library, a revolver close by on the floor.

The police had to break open the door, because the only key to the library's one door was always kept by Pinlever personally. They found it in a pocket of his jacket, which was hanging on a chair near his desk.

The windows were securely locked on the inside. And though the transom over the door was unfastened, it opened no wider than about four inches (10cm). The door did not lock automatically: a key was needed to lock or unlock it.

At the time of the murder, three other people were living at Waverly Mansion. They were: Norbert, the penniless playboy nephew of the wealthy Pinlever, who had come out for the weekend; Williams, Pinlever's valet and chauffeur, and Mrs. Danvers, the housekeeper.

Sergeant Zupp met Inspector Ketchum in the hall on his arrival.

"Thanks for getting here so quickly, Inspector," he said. "As you know, we had Pinlever's body removed because we were sure it was a case of suicide. The room being locked from the inside, and the only key being in Pinlever's jacket pocket, it seemed the obvious conclusion. I was here when they broke the door open, so I can fill in any missing details. Let's go into the library. Nothing has been disturbed."

"What made you suspicious?" asked the Inspector, when the Sergeant closed the library door behind them.

"Little things that came up in conversation with the housekeeper," said the Sergeant. "For example, Pinlever always liked to wear a flower in his buttonhole, and cut a fresh one himself every morning. When we went in, the rose she saw him wearing before she went shopping at nine o'clock, was in the wastebasket. His jacket was as you see it, hanging on the chair, but Mrs. Danvers says he usually hung it on the stand in the corner."

"What about the movements of everybody, leading up to your arrival?" asked the Inspector.

"As the housekeeper was passing the library door to go shopping, Pinlever came out and asked her to get him some cigarettes. At the time, Williams was in the garage tinkering with a noisy backfiring car. Norbert had gone for a walk and said he'd be back around noon. When the housekeeper came back, about an hour later, Williams was still in the garage, but it was quiet. She went to the library with the cigarettes, but got no answer when she knocked. Williams eventually phoned us at the station."

"Where is the nephew?"

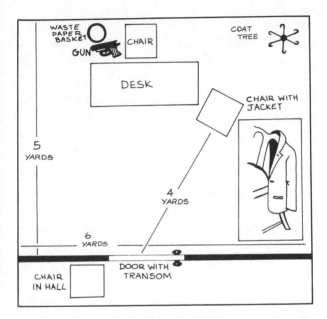

"He hasn't returned yet. He phoned from somewhere to say he was eating out and would be back tonight. Williams is in the garage. When I saw him earlier, he was trying to remove a thorn from his thumb. He said he got it while he was cutting a rose for Pinlever's buttonhole. Mrs. Danvers is annoyed at him because yesterday when Williams wanted some cotton thread to wrap around the handle of one of his tools, she lent him a full spool and he returned it with half of it gone."

"About how much would that be?" asked the Inspector.

"She showed me the spool. Its full length, according to the label, was 25 yards."

"What about motive, Sergeant?" asked Inspector Ketchum.

"Mrs. Danvers, none that I know of. Mr. Williams always seems to have money troubles of some sort, and once told Mrs. Danvers that Pinlever left him something in his will. The nephew is always broke and could expect to inherit everything when his uncle died."

"Do we know anything about the gun?"

"Nothing," said the Sergeant. "We don't even know yet if it belonged to Pinlever."

He tore a page out of his notebook and handed it to the Inspector. "I made this sketch of the scene and I've put in a few measurements. I have a strong feeling that it's murder and Williams did it, but how he made it look like suicide I can't even guess."

"I think you're right," said the Inspector. "But as to how he made it look like Pinlever killed himself, the rose in the wastebasket and one of those measurements give me the answer."

Do you see how he did it?

Solution on pages 314–315.

2
PICTURE PUZZLE MYSTERIES

Art Fake 1

ARTIST BEN FAKINNEM makes copies of the paintings of popular artists and sells them to crooked dealers, who pass them off as originals. Unfortunately for Ben and for the dealers, Ben usually works from his own rough sketches, using his imagination (which is not very good). This leads to careless mistakes that make his fakes fairly easy to detect. In a horse-race picture he copied once, none of the horses had reins for the jockeys to hold onto.

Which of these pictures is the fake?

If you have trouble telling, try looking at them through a magnifying glass.

Solution on pages 315–316.

Art Fake 2

WHICH OF THESE PICTURES is Ben Fakinnem's copy—and which is the original? Remember,

if you have trouble telling, check with a magnifying glass.

Solution on page 316.

Art Fake 3

WHICH SCREEN IS Ben Fakinnem's copy and which is the original?

Solution on page 316.

Art Fake 4

WHICH PICTURE IS Ben Fakinnem's copy and which is the original?

Solution on page 316.

Only Two Cars

THE LOCAL POLICE STATION received an urgent call from Waverly Mansion. It had been robbed. The thieves' car had just driven away and was believed to be heading for the thruway.

The police had only two cars available, but after a quick look at their wall map, they were off at full speed to block roads at two separate points. They knew that these road blocks would prevent the thieves getting to the thruway.

Which two points did they need to block?

Solution on pages 316–317.

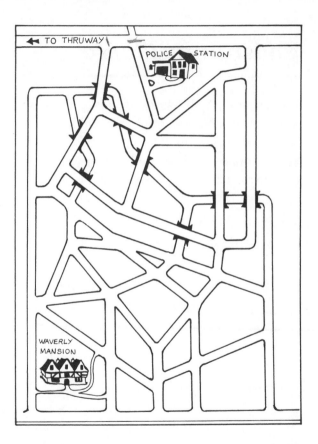

Under Surveillance

THE POLICE HAVE SWIFTY MORAN under observation. A police photographer set up his camera
in a neighboring building that looked out over
Swifty's garage, and he took a series of photos,
which you can see on the opposite page.

Unfortunately, the processors sent the photos back in the wrong sequence.

Can you put them in the right order?

Solution on page 317.

Open Windows at Scotland Yard

DETECTIVE DONNA DiANSA was visiting Scotland Yard on her vacation. She watched as the police artist finished a set of drawings that pictured the chief incidents in a recent robbery.

Suddenly a gust of wind from the open window swept all the papers off the table. The detective helped the artist gather them together, but she laid them down on the table in the order in which they were picked up.

Can you work out the correct sequence?

Solution on page 317.

41

3

SHERLOCK HOLMES

Moriarty's List

"HERE'S A LIST OF THE HOUSE numbers that Professor Moriarty has broken into on Baker Street on consecutive nights, Holmes," said Watson, passing the list to Holmes. "I wonder where he'll strike tonight."

Holmes studied the list for a moment and quickly supplied Watson with an answer. From the list of house numbers below, can you give the number of the house that Moriarty intended to rob that night?

Previous houses robbed: 5, 20, 24, 6, 2, 8, ?

Solution on page 318.

44

Time of Death

SOMETIME AFTER 10 P.M. during a party at Lord Fanshaw's residence, the house was plunged into darkness momentarily. During this time, a shot rang out, and when the lights came back on, Lord Fanshaw was found dead on the floor. Sherlock Holmes arrived at the residence before midnight.

"Can you recall the time of the incident?" Holmes asked one of the guests.

The guest glanced at the clock and informed Holmes that the clock must have stopped at the time of the shooting as the hands of the clock were in exactly the same position now as they had been then. This was not the case. The hands had actually changed places.

1. *Can you tell what time the shooting took place?*

2. *Can you tell what time it was when Holmes asked the guest the question?*

Solution on page 318.

The Secret Club

SHERLOCK HOLMES RECEIVED an urgent telegram from an old friend. The man felt certain that his life was in danger. Holmes and Watson hurried to his lodgings only to find that they were too late. The man had been murdered minutes before they had arrived.

"I found him lying there," said the land lady. "Before he died, he muttered something about belonging to a secret club and quoted the number 92."

"Confounded strange thing to say, Holmes," said Watson.

Holmes nodded his agreement. "Did he say

anything else?" he asked the landlady.

"I asked him who had done this terrible thing, but he just repeated the number 92!" she answered.

Holmes thanked her for her help and dismissed her. He searched the dead man's room. He came across a letter addressed to the man that was from the other three members of the secret club. Their names were Wilson, Updike, and Brown. At the top left of the letter was the name of the dead man, Smith (Code 69). From this, Holmes deduced that he had been murdered by another member of the club, and that the number 92 was in fact the code number of the murderer.

Holmes was then quickly able to supply the name of the killer. Can you?

Solution on page 318.

The Stolen Bracelet

"**I'm baffled,**" said Daphne Ashton-James to Sherlock Holmes. "One of my four servants must have stolen my gold bracelet. I've questioned each of them, but I'm none the wiser.

Branson, my butler, says that Smythe the gardener did it, while Mary the maid says Smythe told her that Branson did it. Smythe told me Bransom did it, and Wilson, the handyman, said he knew which one was the thief but did not wish to say."

Mrs. Ashton-James sighed, and then continued, "I've known Branson and Smythe for many years and I've never known either of them to tell the truth."

Sherlock Holmes smiled as he filled his pipe. "Assuming that the butler and the gardener have not changed their ways, and that Mary and Wilson are telling the truth, it is quite a simple task to deduce which one is the thief," he said.

Can you work out which one of the staff stole the bracelet?

Solution on page 318.

Message from Moriarty

"TAKE A LOOK AT THIS, WATSON," said Holmes, as he passed a coded message to his colleague.

The message read:

TO SHERLOCK HOLMES

T5M5RR5W4w4LLST32LTH3CR5WNJ3W3LST
H 4SW4LLB3MYGR32T3STTR46MPH

                                    MORIARTY

"What does it all mean, Holmes?" exclaimed Watson.

"To find that out, Watson, we must break the code. The numbers obviously represent letters."

"But he doesn't use the numbers one or zero, Holmes," said Watson.

"That is simply because they could be mistaken for the letters I and O, Watson," said Holmes, as he set about breaking the code.

Can you decipher the message?

Solution on page 318.

Witnesses to Murder

SHERLOCK HOLMES was questioning three men who had been witness to a murder,

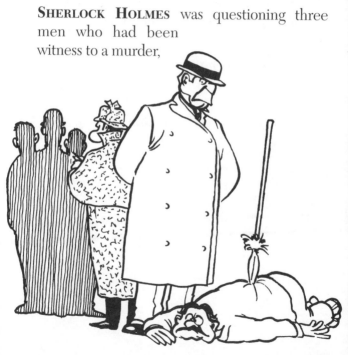

Messrs. Franks, Richards, and Andrews.

Holmes remarked to Mr. Richards on this.

"Yes, I notice that as well," Richards replied. "But none of us have the first name that matches our surname. My first name happens to be Andrew."

Can you give the full name of all three witnesses?

Solution on page 319.

Moriarty's Statement

AT LONG LAST Sherlock Holmes had brought Professor Moriarty to trial for a capital offense. As Holmes looked on, sitting in the back of the courtroom, the judge was about to pronounce

sentence. Moriarty interrupted the judge in mid-sentence and asked to make one more statement. The Judge agreed and gave him the following choice: if his statement was true he would be hanged; if it was false he would be shot by firing squad. A wry smile crossed the face of Sherlock Holmes as Moriarty made a statement that made it impossible to execute him.

What did Moriarty say?

Solution on page 319.

The Death of Foxley

SHERLOCK HOLMES and Doctor Watson stood looking down at the dead body of Lord Foxley.

"I wonder what time he was murdered," said Watson.

At that moment, his Lordship's somewhat forgetful butler stepped forward. "I know exactly when he was murdered," he announced. "I was in my bathroom shaving when I heard the shot. I recall looking in my mirror and the time on the clock behind me said 20 minutes to 10."

What was the correct time of his Lordship's death?

Solution on page 319.

The Dungeon

SHERLOCK HOLMES was being held prisoner in a dark dungeon by the evil Professor Moriarty.

He found 64 candle stubs lying on the dungeon floor. He realized that he could make one full candle from four stubs, and one candle would burn down to a stub in one hour. Working on the theory that Holmes could only light full candles, how many hours of candlelight would he have before being left in total darkness?

Solution on page 319.

The Inheritance

FOLLOWING LORD SMEDHURST'S untimely
death, Sherlock Holmes was given the task of
tracking down his three long lost sons. His
Lordship had left a total of £2,750,000, to be

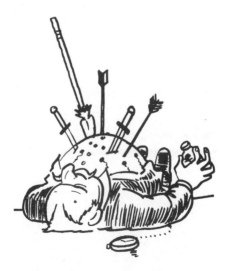

divided among the three of them. His will stated that James, the oldest, was to receive three times as much as John, the youngest, while Clive was to receive half the sum allocated to James.

How much would the three sons each receive?

Solution on page 319.

How Much Poison?

SHERLOCK HOLMES arrested the butler of the Westwood mansion for poisoning the entire Westwood family. After confessing, the butler

went on to explain to Holmes just exactly how it was done.

He filled a wine glass half full of wine, and another glass twice the size one-third full of water. He then topped up each glass with poison before pouring the contents of both glasses into an empty wine decanter.

Can you deduce how much of the mixture was wine and how much was poison?

Solution on page 319.

The Post Office Robbery

THREE MEN WERE being held in custody following a post office robbery in which cash, postal orders, and stamps were stolen, and a teller was shot and killed.

Before being interviewed, the three men agreed to mix up their statements—lies and truth together—to avoid revealing which one of them had actually fired the shot that killed the teller. One of the three was a bad liar, so it was agreed that he should tell the truth at all times. Another would tell one true fact and one lie, while the third would tell lies on all occasions.

Unknown to the three criminals, Sherlock Holmes had overheard this part of their conversation. So when he joined Inspector Lestrade for

the interviews, he was able to announce just who
the killer was. Can you?

The three conflicting statement made by the
robbers were:

DRUMMOND: I collected the cash. Fry shot the
    teller.

FRY: Clark collected the stamps and postal orders. Drummond shot the teller.

CLARK: Fry shot the teller. I collected the cash.

Solution on page 319-320.

The Ransom Note

WHEN LADY SHARP reported the kidnapping of her young son to Sherlock Holmes, Holmes knew that the crime could have been carried out only by one man—Professor Moriarty.

Lady Sharp produced a ransom note for £100,000. The note also carried a warning that should the money not be paid, she would never see her son alive again. As Lady Sharp left 221b Baker Street, a note was delivered by hand to Sherlock Holmes.

"Blast!" cried Holmes, as he read the note before passing it to Dr. Watson. "Moriarty knows that we are on the case, Watson. We must act quickly if we are to save the life of Lady Sharp's son."

Watson read the note. "I don't understand, Holmes. This note is nothing more than gobbledegook."

"Not so, Watson," cried Holmes as he grabbed his coat. "Unless we find Moriarty's hiding place quickly, we will be too late to find the boy alive."

The note read:

HATED HALLS TEAK STREAM HARPS TOADY!

Can you decipher it?

Solution on page 320.

4
SHERMAN HOLMES

NO ONE KNEW where Sherman Oliver Holmes came from or how he'd gotten his money. One day, Capital City was just your run-of-the-mill metropolitan area. The next day, a short, rotund millionaire in a deerstalker cap began showing up at crime scenes, claiming to be the great-great-grandson of Sherlock Holmes and offering his expert opinion.

Sergeant Gunther Wilson of the Major Crimes Division was irritated by how often this eccentric little man with the Southern drawl would appear within minutes of a grisly murder and stick his nose into official police business.

What disturbed Wilson even more was the fact that this eccentric little man was nearly always right.

So Sergeant Wilson decided to swallow his pride and befriend the exasperating, unique little gentleman who would pop up like a fat rabbit and do the work of an entire detective squad.

The Missing Monet

SHERMAN HOLMES didn't know how he did it—but he did, and on a regular basis. Sometimes he'd see a police cruiser and stop to see what was happening. Sometimes he'd follow the sound of a siren. More often than not, he would just be walking or driving around Capital City when a sixth sense would tell him to turn here or stop there.

It was this sixth sense for crime that brought him to the Hudson Office Building on a blustery March day. Sherman settled quietly into a chair in the lobby, patiently waiting for something to happen.

The first visitor to catch his eye was a bike messenger, arriving with a package-filled backpack and a long document tube. The messenger disappeared into an express elevator labeled 31st floor. Five minutes later, the messenger reappeared and left the building, still carrying the tube, but one package lighter. Taking his place in the elevator was an elegantly attired man, an older gentleman, using a cane as he limped heavily on his left leg.

The gentleman reappeared in the lobby ten minutes later. On his exit from the elevator he nearly collided with a woman in a Gucci suit. The umbrella in her left hand became momentarily entangled with the cane in his right.

"Watch where you're going," she snapped.

"My apologies," he replied.

The man limped off and the woman pressed her button and fidgeted with her umbrella until the elevator door closed. Her visit lasted five minutes.

Sherman was beginning to think his crime-sensing instincts were flawed. Perhaps it was this nasty cold he was just getting over. Then a pair of police officers rushed into the lobby and took the same express elevator to the 31st floor.

"It's about time they called the police," Sherman said with satisfaction.

When they left the building a half hour later,

Sherman followed them to the Baker Street Coffee Shop. He slipped into the booth behind theirs, quietly ordered an English muffin, and eavesdropped.

"What was a million-dollar painting doing in the reception area?" the older cop asked his partner. Sherman recognized him as Sergeant Gunther Wilson, an officer he'd chatted with at dozens of other crime scenes.

The 31st floor, it seems, contained the offices of the Hudson Company's top brass, and the furnishings in the reception area included a small Monet oil, about one foot square. Only three visitors had been alone there long enough to cut the painting out of its frame: a bike messenger delivering documents, the ne'er-do-well uncle of the company president wanting to borrow a few dollars, and the vice president's estranged wife, who had come to complain about her allowance. All three had visited the offices before and could have previously noticed the unguarded painting.

"Excuse me," Sherman said, as he rose from his booth and ambled up to Officer Wilson and his partner.

Wilson saw the pudgy little man in his deer-stalker cap and frock-coat and beamed. "Sherlock Holmes, I presume."

"That was my great-great-grandfather," Sherman answered politely. "But I did inherit a few of his modest powers. Would you like me to tell you who stole that painting?"

Who stole the painting?

What clue gave the thief away?

Solution on page 320.

The Pointing Corpse

WHEN THE DETECTIVE BUSINESS was slow the great Sherlock Holmes had spent the long, empty hours playing the violin. Sherman Holmes did the same, but with less soothing results.

"Maybe I should take lessons," he would think as he sawed back and forth across the strings. When things got really slow, Sherman switched on one of his police band radios.

After two boring days of drizzle and inactivity, the detective intercepted a call reporting a murder victim found in a car. Sherman happened to be driving his classic Bentley at the time and made a quick turn up High Canyon Road.

He arrived to find Gunther Wilson standing between his patrol car and a white sedan parked beside a panoramic view. The Sergeant actually looked glad to see him.

"I'm a little out of my depth on this one," he said. "It's a celebrity, Mervin Hightower. Shot at close range. I'm waiting for forensics and a tow truck. On top of his being murdered, his car battery's dead."

The whole city knew Mervin Hightower, a newspaper columnist who specialized in scandalous exposés. Sherman walked around to the driver's side. An arm extended out the partially open window, propped up on the glass edge. The hand was made into a fist, except for the index finger, which was straight and firm with rigor mortis.

He appears to be pointing," Sherman deduced. "How long has the fellow been dead?"

"What do I look like, a clock? The forensics boys will narrow it down. I saw the car and stopped to see if he needed help, which he doesn't. I recognized him, even with the blood."

Sherman looked in to see the columnist's

familiar face contorted and frozen in agony. "I presume the man survived for a minute after the attack. What do you think he was pointing at, old bean? Something that could identify his killer? Sherman lined up his eyes along the extended arm. "What story was he working on?"

Wilson pulled a newspaper from his back pocket. "Here. In today's column, he says he's going to expose some embezzlement from the City Charity Board."

"There are only three people on the Charity Board," Sherman said, checking the column for their names. "Marilyn Lake, Arthur Curtis, and Tony Pine." Then he examined the view: a glistening lake, a neon sign for Curtis Furniture, and a majestic grove of evergreens. "Zounds!"

"Zounds is right. If Mervin was trying to point out his killer, he did a lousy job."

"Not necessarily," Sherman was thinking. "I think he did just fine."

Who killed Mervin Hightower?

How did Sherman know?

Solution on page 321.

All in the Family

SERGEANT WILSON enjoyed an occasional breakfast with Sherman at the Baker Street Coffee Shop. What he didn't enjoy were the homicide calls that so often came right in the middle of the meal. He was just finishing his Belgian waffle with fruit when this morning's call took him to Gleason & Son Insurance, located on a lonely stretch of highway. As usual, Sherman tagged along.

A uniformed officer met them in the parking lot. "The victim is Gary Lovett," the officer told them. "A Gleason & Son employee. That's Neal Gleason and his sister, Patty Lovett. She's the victim's widow." He pointed to an anxious-looking duo, both in their late twenties. "Mr. Gleason discovered the body at about 8:30 A.M."

Neal Gleason stepped forward. His statement sounded rehearsed. "When I pulled into

the parking lot, I saw Gary's car. Gary is often here early, though he's always gone before noon. If Gary wasn't Patty's husband, Dad would've fired him long ago. The front door was open. Right inside the door I saw him, like that."

Wilson examined the body in the doorway. The man's head was a bloody mess, and it took the sergeant a while to realize that the rifle now bagged as evidence had been used as a blunt instrument, its wooden stock having been slammed into his head like a baseball bat. The body was cold and rigor mortis had already come and gone.

"That's my husband's rifle," volunteered the widow. "He kept it here at the office. Last night at home, Gary got this phone call. He said he had to go to the office and that I should just go to bed. I thought he might be going to see another woman. This morning when I woke up he was still gone. So I went to find him. I must have arrived here just a minute after my brother did."

"I think we should probably call Dad," Neal said.

That call wouldn't be necessary, for at that exact moment, George Gleason was pulling into the parking lot. The burly insurance broker eased himself out of his Cadillac and wordlessly took in the scene, the body, the bagged rifle, and his two children.

Patty ran up to him. "Someone murdered Gary," she moaned. "The police suspect us, Neal and me."

Gleason hugged his daughter, exchanged glances with his son, then turned to face Sergeant Wilson. "I killed him," he said softly and simply. "I met him here last night and shot him, right in the head. My kids had nothing to do with it."

As the uniform took Gleason's statement, Wilson stepped off to the side with Sherman.

"You don't have to tell me," Wilson whispered.

"I picked up on the clue, too."

"Perhaps, old man," Sherman said with a smile. "But did you pick up on the right clue?"

Who killed Gary Lovett?

What clue points to the killer?

Solution on pages 321–322.

An Alarming Jewel Heist

"**MAYBE NOW** you'll stop bugging me," Zach Alban said as Sherman walked into his friend's shop. "See? I got that alarm system you recommended, wired straight to the police station."

"It's about time," Sherman replied. Alban Jewelers had just expanded its business and finally had some jewels worth stealing.

"Mr. Alban, I'm leaving now." Ricky Mayfield had finished clearing out the window displays, placing the felts of precious stones into their locked drawers for the night. The door buzzed as the young assistant raced out to catch his bus.

Melanie, Alban's second in command, was putting on her jacket and looking at the newly installed alarm panel. "Are you sure you don't want to give me the code, Zach? That way you won't always have to be here to open and close."

"Not right now. Maybe in a few days when I get more used to it."

"Whatever," Melanie said. A rumbling from the street announced the arrival of her boyfriend's motorcycle. "See you tomorrow." And she was quickly out the door, hopping onto the back of a Harley-Davidson.

Zach led the way into the back office, eager

to show his friend the entire system. "Once I set the code, any broken window or open door will trigger the alarm. Twenty seconds, that's all the time I have to disarm it. Sam, why don't you go home, too?"

Sam Wells switched off the computer and wished his boss a good night. Seconds later they heard the front door buzz, signaling the last employee's departure. "Want to help me close up?" Zach asked Sherman. "I don't want to make a mistake. After your first false alarm, they start charging you a fine."

Sherman and Zach followed the instructions to the letter, then went down the block to Gil's Tavern. When they left an hour later, Sherman noticed a police patrol car parked in front of Alban Jewelers.

"Break-in and burglary," an officer informed the devastated storeowner. "The back alley window was smashed. We responded within two minutes. But the alley was empty and the crooks were already gone."

Sherman was surprised by the thoroughness of the burglary. The jewel drawers had been chiseled open and stripped of their contents. The display cases had also been broken into and ransacked, glass shards littering the hard-wood floor.

"So much for my brand new alarm system," Zach said almost accusingly.

"Not so fast," Sherman said. "If it weren't for the alarm system I wouldn't know who the burglar is."

Who robbed the shop?

How did Sherman know?

Solution on page 322-323.

Trick or Treat

SHERMAN LOVED HALLOWEEN. It gave him a chance to dress up as Sherlock Holmes and still seem normal. The pudgy detective was in his usual costume, escorting a squadron of children down Elm Street when he noticed a crowd gathering in front of old Miss Cleghorn's house. "She must be up to her usual," chortled Sherman. "Putting on some horrific mask and scaring the kids at the door."

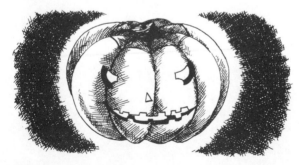

Miss Cleghorn was indeed scaring the kids, but not intentionally. Inside the open door, Sherman could see her frail body lying in the entry hall, wearing a monster mask, her head surrounded by blood. A plastic bowl lay nearby, its contents of wrapped candy strewn everywhere.

Sergeant Wilson stood beside the body. He glanced over at the man with the calabash pipe and deerstalker cap. "Is that a costume, Holmes? With you it's hard to tell."

"What happened, my respectable partner in crime?"

"It's an accident. It took us a while to reconstruct what happened." Wilson pointed up to where a strand of large pearls lay centered at the top of the steps. "She was upstairs when the first trick-or-treaters rang the bell. She put on the mask and grabbed the bowl. She must have slipped on the pearls and tumbled down the stairs."

Two cars pulled up at the curb, one behind the other. Sherman recognized Miss Cleghorn's niece and nephew, Emma and Bobby, as they got out of their cars and approached the front door, both dressed for a night out and seemingly unaware of the tragedy.

"Aunt Rita," Bobby gasped.

"Your aunt had an accident," Sergeant Wilson told them. "She's dead. The kids had been coming up to the door for half an hour or so and getting no answer. One of them finally looked through the window and saw her."

Bobby noticed the spilled candy and the mask. "What's she doing wearing a mask?"

"She was obviously doing her Halloween thing," Emma said.

"She promised she wouldn't this year. We were taking her out to dinner."

"Well, obviously she changed her mind," Emma said, shaking her head. "I don't know how many times I told her not to wear a mask on the stairs."

"When did you last see your aunt?" asked Sherman.

Bobby stared at the rather over-age trick or treater "Uh, I dropped by this morning. My daughter left her skateboard here. Aunt Rita made me coffee and we chatted."

Sergeant Wilson grabbed Sherman by the collar and dragged him aside. "Don't try to make this a murder. The neighbors say there were no visitors since this morning."

"Someone could have driven up the back alley and come in that way," argued Sherman. "Believe me, friend, this was murder."

Why couldn't it have been accidental?

Whom does Sherman suspect and why?

Solution on page 323.

5

DR. J.L. QUICK-SOLVE

DR. JEFFREY LYNN QUICKSOLVE, professor of criminology, retired from the police force as a detective at a very young age. Now he works with various police departments and private detectives as a consultant when he is not teaching at the university.

He certainly knows his business, solving crimes. Many people are amazed at how he solves so many crimes so quickly. When asked how he does it, he replies, "I'm no smarter than anyone else. I just listen very well."

Brotherly Love

TOM AND PAT PENNYSWORTH were extremely wealthy brothers. Tom had been missing for two days. Dr. J.L. Quicksolve was at their house talking to Pat.

"When did you last see your brother?" Dr. Quicksolve asked.

"Saturday afternoon, around two o'clock, a tall blond woman came here to pick him up. I guess they had a date. They drove away in her car, and I haven't seen Tom since then," Pat explained.

Just then, the phone rang and Pat answered it.

"It's for you," he said, handing the phone to Quicksolve.

"J.L. Quicksolve," he said into the phone.

"Dr. Quicksolve," came the response, "this is Office Dennis. We've found the body of Tom Pennysworth out here at his cottage on Silver Lake. He's been shot to death.

"Any clues, Office Dennis?" Quicksolve asked.

"No, we're still looking."

"Let me know right away if you find anything. Good-bye."

"What is it?" Pat Pennysworth asked as the detective hung up the phone and turned to him.

"I'm afraid it's bad news. Your brother's been

found. He's dead," said Dr. Quicksolve.

"Oh, no!" Pat cried.

"Where were you on Saturday evening, Pat?"

"I was right here! You can't suspect me! I didn't go anywhere near the cottage!" Pat shouted.

"I think you did, Pat," Dr. Quicksolve stated coolly.

Why does he suspect the brother?

Solution on page 324.

Flying Thief

DR. J.L. QUICKSOLVE was flying out to Colorado to visit his aunt and uncle. He had been talking to the lady beside him, Miss Pettithief, for quite some time. When she learned that he was a detective, she was eager to share her story with him.

"I was so upset after the robbery that I had to take time off and take vacation," she explained.

"Tell me about the robbery," Dr, Quicksolve said.

"I was the only teller on duty at my bank at the time. The thing is, the robbery happened just at the time we had a power failure. A man walked up to my window and handed me a note that said to hand over the money, and that he had a gun. I stepped on the silent alarm, but apparently nothing happened because the electricity had gone out. So the man got away," she told the detective.

"Did they catch the robber?" Quicksolve asked.

"No, he got away. They did get a picture of him on the bank's security camera, but the camera just showed my back and the top of his head. It didn't even show me handing over the money, but I could see enough in the video to tell it was the robber."

"Was the robber someone you had seen before?" Dr. Quicksolve asked.

"No, I had never seen him before, but I did give a description," Miss Pettithief said.

"I bet the thief is about your height, your weight, with your hair and eye color. Am I right? Quicksolve asked.

Why does he suspect her?

Solution on page 324.

Jacked Up

DR. J.L. QUICKSOLVE was awakened by the sound of his dog barking downstairs in the front hall by the door. He jumped out of bed and looked out his window to see his car jacked up

on one side, and two young men trying to remove his wheel. Quicksolve opened the window and shouted at the two men. They ran to their car, backed out, and sped away as Quicksolve dashed to the phone and called the police station. They had a car in the area and called it immediately.

Quicksolve slipped on his pants and ran downstairs and outside. He had just finished examining his car when the police car turned into the drive. There were two officers in the front seat and two other men in the back seat. When the police car came to a halt, the driver got out and walked over to Dr. Quicksolve.

"We caught these two speeding away from the area as soon as we got the call. We searched the car, but we didn't find any evidence we can use," said the officer.

"Did you search the trunk of the car?" asked Dr. Quicksolve.

"Yes, we did. Except for their own spare tire, it was absolutely empty. I don't think we really have anything to hold them on right now."

"Well, I think you do. It's not what you found, but what you didn't find. Arrest them and check for prints later," said Quicksolve.

What evidence was he talking about?

Solution on page 324.

Motorcycle Mischief

DR. J.L. QUICKSOLVE came into the police station to invite his friend Sergeant Rebekah Shurshot, to have lunch. When he walked into her office, he saw a young man and a young woman sitting in chairs and talking with Sergeant Shurshot.

The man was speaking. He had crutches leaning against the chair, and his right knee was bandaged.

"I didn't steal her motorcycle," he was saying. "You can see someone hit me with their car door when I pulled up to a stoplight. He swung his door open and hit my leg right here." He pointed to the bandage. "I only had the one leg on the ground because I had just stopped, and my other foot was on the brake. So I fell over when that door hit me. I was trying to get up when another guy jumped out of the car,

107

108

pushed me down, and took off on the motorcycle. It all happened so fast that I couldn't do anything about it!"

Sergeant Shurshot smiled at Dr. Quicksolve and asked him to sit down. "Marcie," she said to Dr. Quicksolve, indicating the young lady, "was trying to sell her motorcycle. Tom, here, took it for a test ride. But then he called Marcie and told her it had been stolen. Marcie thinks he stole it. I'm trying to get the story about what happened."

"Tom, have you ridden motorcycles much?" Dr. Quicksolve asked the young man.

"Quite a bit, but I've never owned one before. I just finished the Rider's Safety Course, and I got a license. I liked her bike. I probably would have bought it, but I didn't steal it," Tom said.

"I think you did, Tom," Dr. Quicksolve said.

Why doesn't he believe Tom's story?

Solution on page 324.

Murdered Miss

THE WOMAN had been strangled. There were
no witnesses and few clues. Her body was on
the couch in the TV room. Two half-full glasses
of lemonade were on the coffee table beside a
half-empty bowl of popcorn. Dr. J.L.
Quicksolve picked up each glass. The ice cubes
clinked against the glass as he smelled each one
for scent of tobacco, lipstick, or anything that
might be a clue. Nothing. He turned to the
boyfriend, who had called the police. "Tell me
what you know," he said.

"Sharna and I had been sitting here watching
TV, as you can see. I remembered I had some
errands to run, so I left. When I came back, I
found her here like this. Then I called the
police," he explained.

"How long were you gone?" asked Dr.
Quicksolve.

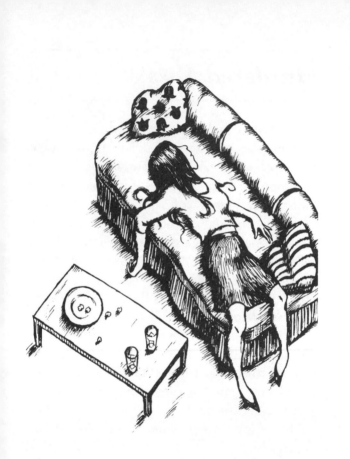

"Oh, I was gone at least two hours. Hey! You don't suspect me, do you? I wouldn't have stayed here and called the police if I had done this. I tell you, I was gone for at least two hours! Anybody could have come in here, and she has an old boyfriend who was pretty jealous when she broke up with him. You'd better question him!"

"We will, certainly, but my guess is that he will have a much better alibi than you have," said Dr. Quicksolve.

Why does Dr. Quicksolve suspect this boyfriend?

Solution on page 324.

Murder
Between Friends

THE BUILDING WAS an old house near the university. It had been divided into four apartments. Its owner, Gracious Host, lived in a large apartment downstairs. She rented out the three apartments upstairs. Dr. J.L. Quicksolve had heard the call over the police radio and arrived before the officers.

Gracious described her tenants to Dr. Quicksolve. She said Tweeter Woofer was a young "hippie type" who sometimes played her music too loudly. "I told her one more complaint and she would be out on the street."
Baby Blossom was hearing impaired, but "she reads lips." Terry Cloth was dead.

Gracious said she was sure only her three tenants were in the building when she heard

the shots and discovered the body.

The hall was quiet when Dr. Quicksolve walked upstairs. The woman in the bathrobe lay against the wall, as if she were taking a nap. The three red stains told him the nap would last forever.

Dr. Quicksolve heard music in the back of

the apartment and smelled burning incense when Tweeter Woofer opened her apartment door to let him enter. Miss Woofer was shocked when he explained what had happened. As they stood inside the door, she said, "This is so upsetting. Who would shoot Terry?" She said she did not hear anything and did not see anything.

Dr. Quicksolve knocked quietly on Baby Blossom's door. She and her dog, a yellow Labrador, came to the door. He explained what had happened.

"I was a little afraid to open the door because I thought I heard shots," she said. "I guess I was right."

When Dr. Quicksolve went back downstairs, the police had arrived. "I have a good suspect," he told them.

Which woman did he suspect?

Solution on pages 324–325.

Jokers Wild

THE SNOW HAD just begun, but the bitter winter wind forced Dr. J.L. Quicksolve to grab his hat with one hand and hold his collar closed with the other as he got out of his VW Beetle and walked past the ice-frosted car in the driveway. He walked carefully up the icy steps to the door of the house.

Miss Forkton opened the door when he rang the bell. He introduced himself and she invited him in.

"It sure is cold out there," he said.

"Too cold for burglars, you would think," came her reply.

"Tell me about your robbery, Miss Forkton," Dr. Quicksolve said as he removed his coat. Miss Forkton took the coat and laid it on top of her own fur coat on a chair next to the phone table.

"Well, I just got home a few minutes ago.

When I came in the door and saw my safe open," she said, pointing to an open wall safe, "I went straight to the phone and called you. I am glad you could get here so fast."

"Yes, we may have a hot trail for such a cold night," Quicksolve mused.

"I had a fortune in jewels stolen, Dr. Quicksolve. I don't think this is a good time for jokes," she said.

"I agree with you one hundred percent. So why did you bring me out on such a cold night for this joke of yours, Miss Forkton?" the detective asked.

Why did he mistrust Miss Forkton?

Solution on page 325.

Threat

IT WAS NOT THE FIRST TIME Dr. J.L. Quicksolve had received a threatening letter. This one, though, seemed a little more menacing than the usual prank. It contained a small piece of plastic that was a bit of casing from a cylinder of dynamite.

Dr. Quicksolve had taken steps to protect himself. He left his VW Beetle parked on the street as a temptation for the would-be bomber. He set up a video camera in his upstairs window to watch his car through the night and keep a taped record.

Others were watching too. Sergeant Rebekah Shurshot drove the unmarked police car through the dark neighborhood. Officer Longarm sat beside her. They were going to drive by Dr. Quicksolve's house "just to see if anything looked suspicious." They knew about

the threat and were worried about their friend.

As they drove closer to the house, they saw a large sedan about half a block behind Dr. Quicksolve's VW. The car was dark. They did not realize it was occupied by two men until they were beside it. The small flame of a lighter flickered up to a cigarette on the passenger's side.

"Let's check this out," Sergeant Shurshot said, pulling up in front of the parked car.

She approached the driver's door. Officer Longarm went around to the other side. The driver's window came down. The smiling mustached driver spoke.

"Hi, we're lost, and we stopped to look at our map," he said, holding a map up to prove his point. "Could you help us out?"

Sergeant Shurshot was not smiling when she said, "Please get out of the car slowly with your hands up."

The two men looked at the officers and their drawn guns and did as they were told.

What tipped off the officers?

Solution on page 325.

Claude Viciously

"**THE RINGMASTER INSISTED** that Claude use the new lion in his act because the animal was so big and aggressive—a crowd pleaser," Mrs. Viciously told Dr. J.L. Quicksolve as they sat in her trailer discussing her husband's death. "The lion wasn't trained. Claude was afraid of him. Claude hadn't been afraid in years, but this scared him. He sat right there, barely two hours ago at breakfast and decided he wouldn't go in with the new lion unless he had his gun loaded. He was always proud that he could work with the big cats without even the blank pistol some trainers use. He was scared. Animals sense that, you know."

Claude's body lay in the center of the ring covered by a blanket. The lion had been put away, and Lieutenant Rootumout and two other men stood beside the body. One man,

obviously the ringmaster, wore a fancy suit with long tails. The other, a performer, wore black tights and a bright red sash.

124

"I should not have insisted he use that new lion," the ringmaster said, clearly shaken by the death.

Lieutenant Rootumout held up a clear plastic bag as Dr. Quicksolve approached. It contained a large revolver. "It's empty," he said to Dr. Quicksolve.

"I can't believe he forgot the bullets," Stretch Prettitight said. "He was afraid of that lion."

Dr. Quicksolve bent down and lifted the edge of the blanket to look at the body. "Looks like murder," he said.

"Lions can't be charged with murder," Stretch scoffed.

"You can," Dr. Quicksolve replied.

Why does Dr. Quicksolve suspect Stretch?

Solution on page 325.

The Mings' Things

AS THEY WALKED AROUND the house, Officer Longarm told Dr. J.L. Quicksolve about the robbery.

"Mary Ming said she often forgets to lock her back door. She said her neighborhood has had very little crime for years, and Inky, her cocker spaniel, would at least bark at a stranger and scare him away. She went to bed late last night, though, and she woke up and found her two antique vases, handed down from her husband's ancestors, were missing. She said they were valuable and very important to her family. There are no signs of forced entry, and nothing else is missing."

Dr. Quicksolve and Officer Longarm went into the kitchen where Marvin and Mary Ming sat sipping coffee. Their friend Jade Greene was consoling Mary.

"No one is going to break anything so valuable," she said. "The police will find . . ."

"Find what?" said a petite red-haired woman who had just come in through the back door. "I saw the police car. What happened?"

Officer Longarm and Dr. Quicksolve looked questioningly at the new arrival.

"This is Diana, my neighbor," Mary Ming said.

Looking through the short hallway at the

empty end of the mantel, Diana cried, "Your vase! Oh, no! Did you have a burglar?" she asked.

"Yes," Mary Ming replied sadly. "We did."

"The police will take care of things," Jade Greene said, continuing to console her friend.

"I'm sure they will find them," Diana added, supporting Jade's confidence. You'll get them back."

"Don't worry, dear," Marvin Ming told his wife, and put his hand on hers.

"Thanks for your confidence," Officer Longarm said.

"Were you green with envy, or just greedy?" Dr. Quicksolve asked.

Who was Dr. Quicksolve talking to? Why?

Solution on pages 325–326.

Roadblock

"LOOKS LIKE SOMEBODY knew they were coming and cut this tree down to block the way so they could overcome the guards and get the money from the bank truck," Officer Longarm told Dr. J.L. Quicksolve and Sergeant Rebekah Shurshot. "I found the driver and guard tied up in the back of the armored truck," he said.

They were about five miles from town. The armored bank truck with one guard and a driver had left the downtown branch of the Bingo National Bank and Trust at six o'clock that morning. The driver and guard stood near Officer Longarm's police car, waiting to answer questions.

"The bank got a call from the driver this morning at six-thirty," Officer Longarm continued. "The driver told them about the tree down over the road. He said it didn't look like anyone

was around, so they would get out and see if
they could move it. The bank said they heard
nothing further, so they called the police. I was
just passing the bank when the message came
over the radio, so I headed out this way. I got
here in five minutes and found this."

Dr. Quicksolve walked around the armored
truck. The doors were wide open, and it was
empty. The tree that lay across the road was
long enough to prevent a large vehicle from
getting past. It was small enough, though, for
two men to be able to drag it out of the way.

"It's funny that the robbers would know which way the bank truck was coming," Sergeant Shurshot said. "They change their route everyday."

"I think they knew as soon as the driver was told," Dr. Quicksolve said, "but they still took their time."

What did Dr. Quicksolve mean?

Solution on page 326.

Brake for Diamonds

TEN MINUTES INTO the Kris Crossing Heritage Festival Bicycle Race, Dr. J.L. Quicksolve was in the middle of the pack. They had started down a steep hill, turned a sharp right at the Kris Crossing Jewelry Store, gone uphill briefly, down a gradual slope, and around a fast sweeping turn that would lead them out of town.

Dr. Quicksolve swept around the wide turn in a sea of riders. Suddenly he was distracted by the sound of police sirens behind him. He worked his way out of the crowd of bicyclists and stopped at the side of the road. He quickly decided to give up the race and pedal back to see what was going on.

As he returned to the curve he'd rounded minutes before, he saw there had been an accident. A rider was adjusting his fanny pack and looking at the blood dripping from his knee and arm.

"I'm all right," the man said. "The front brake didn't work. I need to get going."

Obviously, the injured man had rounded the corner, hit his brakes (there were marks on the pavement), and slammed into the brick wall of Scalper's Barber Shop.

"He flew right over the handlebars," one witness said.

"Then his bike smashed into the wall," said another.

"The whole front section is busted for sure," said a third person, who was down on one knee, looking at the bike.

Dr. Quicksolve reached into a satchel behind the seat of his bike. He called police headquarters to find out what the sirens were all about. "Someone in a raincoat and a ski mask just robbed the Kris Crossing Jewelry Store," Sergeant Rebekah Shurshot told him.

"Was he wearing pants?" Dr. Quicksolve asked.

Why did Dr. Quicksolve ask that question?

Solution on page 326.

Tracks and a Footprint

DR. J.L. QUICKSOLVE and Sergeant Rebekah Shurshot both enjoyed a country ride in the fall and a walk through the woods and fields. But this time the sights nature provided were spoiled by the obviously unnatural demise of the man whose body lay sprawled near two tire tracks on a rise in the sandy field. He had been shot.

"The tire tracks aren't clear enough to get a good print," Lieutenant Rootumout said.

"The tracks are so close to each other," Sergeant Shurshot said, "it must have been a small car."

"The curious thing is that one footprint is in the middle of the tire tracks," Lieutenant Rootumout said. "It's deep, so it must have been a heavy man, but there's only one footprint. It looks like a one-legged man dropped from out of the sky, left this body here, and flew away again."

"Maybe it is the victim's footprint," Sergeant Shurshot said, "and maybe he was pushed out of a plane or helicopter."

"No, it isn't his footprint," Lieutenant Rootumout said. "It's bigger than his shoes. He doesn't look heavy enough to make that impression, and why is there only one footprint?"

Dr. Quicksolve punched his hands into the

pockets of his sportscoat. He looked down at the body, the two parallel tracks, and the one footprint. "Were there any other clues?" he asked.

"We found one nine-millimeter shell on the ground by the footprint, though he obviously has been shot twice—another mystery," Lieutenant Rootumout said. "There are not many vehicles in the area. We've gotten road-blocks set up, and we're inspecting cars. We're hoping for another clue."

Dr. Quicksolve said, "I don't think we're looking for a car, but a search of the vehicle should provide conclusive evidence."

Why not look for a car? What conclusive evidence?

Solution on page 327.

Assault in the Mall

"**THE MALL WAS** just closing when the robbery took place," Sergeant Rebekah Shurshot told Dr. J.L. Quicksolve, who sat across from her in her office. "The victim was a clerk at the Collect-to-Keep Gift Shop at the southwest end of the mall. The thief threatened the clerk, Kent Membermuch. Kent said the man held his hand in his pocket as if he had a gun. He said he would shoot if Kent didn't hand over the money. When Kent gave him the money, the guy pulled an empty hand out of his pocket and hit Kent in the nose. It's broken. Kent is still in the hospital."

"Did he describe the robber?" Dr. Quicksolve asked.

"When I asked him to describe the man, he just said he'd know him if he saw him again. I told him security caught three men leaving the

mall in the area of the gift shop. It almost has to be one of the three. We put the men in a lineup and took pictures of them. I was just going to take them over to the hospital and have Kent look at them."

Sergeant Shurshot handed the three Polaroid snapshots to Dr. Quicksolve. He looked through them quickly. The first man was very tall—about six feet eight inches tall—according to the lines and numbers on the wall behind him in the lineup room. He had a black mustache and short black hair. The second man was about 20 years old. He wore a white blazer with red polka-dots. His hair was in a ponytail tied back behind his head. The third man was about six feet tall and was pretty ordinary-looking.

Dr. Quicksolve shuffled through the pictures again, picked one out, and said, "It's this one."

Which man did Dr. Quicksolve pick?

Solution on page 327.

Sweepen in the Warehouse

SERGEANT REBEKAH SHURSHOT knew Dr. J.L. Quicksolve would be on his way home from teaching at the university when she got the call about a robbery at the Harry Brush Company warehouse. She called him on his cellular phone, and they agreed to meet at the warehouse near the river. Officer Kautchya was on the loading dock with another man when Dr. Quicksolve and Sergeant Shurshot pulled into the parking lot.

The other man turned out to be the night custodian, Don Sweepen. Don took them all inside the dark building as he explained what happened. His keys jingled at his side as he pulled out his long flashlight to light their way down the rows of shelves of boxes.

"The lights went out when I was cleaning," he said. "I checked the fuses. Then I went outside to see if something was wrong with the line. It looked like the electric wire had come down, so I went back in to call about it. When I walked down this row of dog brushes, I

walked right up to some guy trying to get into the safe down there."

He pointed down the row of boxes where his flashlight showed a safe with the door wide open.

"He stood up right in my face when I surprised him. I grabbed him by the shirt, and we struggled for several minutes. Then another guy grabbed me from behind. They tied me up, took the money from the safe, and got away. I got myself untied and called the police."

"Did you get a look at them?" Sergeant Shurshot asked.

"I didn't get a very good look," Don said. "They were big men. Both of them were about my size. They wore coveralls and masks."

"What were your partners' names?" Dr. Quicksolve asked.

Why did Dr. Quicksolve think the thieves were Don Sweepen's partners?

Solution on page 327.

Robbem Blind, Attorneys at Law

Dr. J.L. Quicksolve drove out of the gentle rain-shower as he pulled up to the gate of the parking structure. The parking attendant was just taking the money from Dr. Quicksolve when they both heard a shot that sounded like it came from the upper level of the structure. When they got to the upper level, they found the body of someone who had been shot. No one else was in the area.

"Do you know who it is?" Dr. Quicksolve asked the attendant.

"Yes, it's Greg Robbem. He's a lawyer with Robbem Blind, Attorneys at Law. Their office is in this building," the attendant said.

"Call the police. I'm going to see if anyone is in their office now," Dr. Quicksolve said.

When he got to the law office, he knocked and entered without waiting. One man was there, behind his desk, cleaning up a large puddle of water that had apparently come from the open window.

"Hello," said the detective. "Are you Blind?"

"Why, yes, I am. What is it?" the man answered, blinking nervously.

"I'm Dr. Jeffrey Quicksolve, and I have bad news. Your partner, Mr. Robbem, has just been murdered."

"Oh, no! What happened?" Mr. Blind cried.

"Somebody just shot him in the parking structure," said the detective.

"I see," Mr. Blind said.

"Have you been here long, Mr. Blind?" Dr. Quicksolve asked.

"Yes, I've been sitting right here at my desk for at least an hour. You don't suspect me, do you?" Mr. Blind asked.

"Yes, I'm afraid I do suspect you, Mr. Blind. Your alibi doesn't hold water.

Why doesn't Dr. Quicksolve believe Mr. Blind?

Solution on page 328.

Tied Up at
the Moment

JONATHON ABBELCORE was talking to Officer
Kautchya when Dr. J.L. Quicksolve arrived.
Jonathon was the butler for the Duckets.

"Mr. and Mrs. Ducket are in Europe on hol-
iday," he was explaining. "I've been watching
the house. I went out about two hours ago to
get a few groceries for myself. When I got back
I had just reached the door when a man came
out of the shadows with a gun. He was tall and
thin. I noticed he held the gun in his left hand.
I think it was a .38. He forced me to let him into
the house, brought me into the den, and tied
me up. I heard him ransacking the house for
almost half an hour. He must have been loading
up the Duckets' car, because I heard him go out
and come in several times. Finally I heard the

147

door lock and struggled to get untied, but I couldn't. I was able to get the gag off my mouth and yell out the window. A fellow walking by heard me and ran in here and untied me. My word, I was glad to see him! As soon as I was untied, I got to the phone and called the police."

"Did you know the man who untied you?" Dr. Quicksolve asked.

"No, I've never seen him before, and he left when he saw I was all right," Jonathon answered.

"I'm afraid you've tied yourself up in lies, Mr. Abbelcore," Dr. Quicksolve said.

Why does Dr. Quicksolve think Jonathon is lying?

Solution on page 328.

Fire Liar

CAPTAIN REELUMIN switched on the red flashing light attached to his dashboard and sounded his siren as he made a quick turnaround and sped away. He and Dr. J.L. Quicksolve had been on their way to question a suspect when they got a message about a house on fire.

They arrived right behind two fire trucks and

a squad car. Another police car came up behind them. The driver turned off his siren and two policemen got out. The back half of the house was in flames that reached up over the roof. Firemen came out the front door dragging a body. When he realized the man had been shot through the chest, Captain Reelumin began his investigation.

After the fire had been put out, an arson investigator arrived. He explained how a fire-bomb had been used to start the fire near the

back porch. Captain Reelumin had his men question the next-door neighbors while he and Dr. Quicksolve went to the house directly across the street.

They rang the doorbell and waited several minutes before a man finally peeked out the window. He opened the door and stood there in his pajamas.

Captain Reelumin showed his badge and said, "Sorry to bother you, but we would like to ask you a few questions about the fire."

Looking across the street at all the trucks, the man said, "Wow! I don't know anything about a fire. You just woke me up. I work nights and sleep in, but sure, I'd be glad to answer any questions."

"Why did you murder your neighbor?" Dr. Quicksolve asked him.

Why did Dr. Quicksolve suspect the man?

Solution on page 328.

If Fish Could Talk

DR. J.L. QUICKSOLVE was eating donuts at the Donut Shop with Officer Longshot and a few local friends, when a call came over Officer Longshot's portable radio. There had been a murder nearby. Dr. Quicksolve took his donut with him.

The manager let Dr. Quicksolve and Officer Longshot into a large, expensive apartment on the eighth floor of the huge apartment building. The apartment was a mess. Kitchen cupboards were open. Dishes were broken and scattered. Cushions from the couch were on the floor. Chairs were turned over. Rock music came from the stereo, and the body of a man lay in the middle of the floor. A knife was in his back. Two goldfish were circling monotonously in a small, clear fishbowl, ignoring the outside world.

"If they could only talk," Officer Longshot said.

The manager, Mr. Keyperson, said, "He's Donald Deadman. He's lived here for several

years. I found him like this a few minutes ago. He was planning to go to Chicago tomorrow with his friend who had been here for several days. He wanted me to keep an eye on things, water his plants and stuff. I was going to ask him about it. When he didn't answer the door, I thought he might have left early. I came in to see if he had gone already. It looks like he caught a burglar in the act."

"Do you know who his friend is?" Dr. Quicksolve asked.

"Yes, I have his name and his license number. We try to keep track of overnight visitors."

"Good," Dr. Quicksolve said. "Have the Chicago police track him down," he said to Officer Longarm. "This wasn't a burglary."

How does Dr. Quicksolve know this was not a normal burglary?

Solution on page 328.

Baubles

AN OLD-FASHIONED BELL rang out when Dr. J.L Quicksolve turned the knob and opened the door to the old jewelry store. The store owner, Berry Opal, greeted Dr. Quicksolve with a handshake. The jeweler suspected his clerk after the third robbery in six months. All three robberies had taken place while this same clerk was working alone in the jewelry store. Mr. Opal asked Dr. Quicksolve to question him.

"After the first two robberies," the clerk explained to Dr. Quicksolve, "I decided to bring my gun to work. I'm pretty good with a pistol, and I wear it here under my jacket. I just did not get a chance to use it. The thief had a gun, or at least he said he did. He had his hand in his pocket, and I couldn't take a chance with his hand already on his gun like that. If I had any chance to get the drop on him, I would

have stopped this robbery and saved my job! I'll never forget what he looked like: tall, bald-headed, with a big handlebar mustache. I'll probably be fired now, even though I didn't have anything to do with the robbery. It's just been bad luck that I've been here when the place gets robbed."

"I understand the thief got away with quite a lot this time," Dr. Quicksolve commented.

"Yeah, two large bags of jewels! He could hardly carry it all, but he wasn't about to let go of them. We had just recently replenished our stocks from the last robbery. We were even stocked up extra for a sale," the clerk explained. "I don't know what I'll do if I lose this job!"

"At least you'll have a place to stay and three square meals a day," Dr. Quicksolve said.

What did Dr. Quicksolve mean?

Solution on pages 328–329.

Woof! Woof!
Bang! Bang!

THE BODY OF SHIRLEY STONEDEAD lay face down on the stairs. One arm stretched up to the stair above her head. It almost looked as if she had fallen asleep on the stairs, except for the three bullet holes in her back. At the bottom of the steps lay a pit bull terrier. It had taken two bullets to stop the dog.

The police photographer was taking pictures as a tall man in a flashy suit, Barrie Scarrie, talked to Dr. J.L. Quicksolve and Sergeant Rebekah Shurshot. The long scar on the man's face seemed to make a smile impossible. "I had an early appointment with Miss Stonedead. She owed me money. I came to pick it up," Barrie said. "As I was just about to push the doorbell, I heard a dog bark and two shots. Then I heard a noise in the back of the house, and a car came backing out of the driveway and took off. I didn't see the driver, and I didn't recognize the car. The door of the house was unlocked, so I went in. I saw Miss Stonedead and her dead dog. I called the police. That's all I know."

Have you known Miss Stonedead long?" Dr. Quicksolve asked.

"Yes, I have. I used to work here. I was her bodyguard," Barrie explained.

Dr. Quicksolve and Sergeant Shurshot stepped aside to listen to what Officer Longarm had found out. "The back door was broken open. A safe upstairs was jimmied open too. It's empty," Officer Longarm said. "It had to be a burglar. Did Mr. Scarrie give you a description of the suspect?" Officer Longarm asked Sergeant Shurshot.

"No," Sergeant Shurshot answered, "but I imagine he has a picture of the murderer in his wallet." Dr. Quicksolve chuckled at her little joke.

What did Sergeant Shurshot mean?

Solution on page 329.

B.B. Bigstuff

WE ARRESTED Bobby Bluntnose, the private detective, for murdering B.B. Bigstuff, the men's clothing tycoon. Then we had to let him go," Lieutenant Rootumout told Dr. J.L. Quicksolve as they sat in Dr. Quicksolve's library sipping coffee. "He had the motive. He had worked for B.B. Bigstuff as a security guard and was recently fired for making fun of short people. Remember, B.B. Bigstuff was only five-foot-one, but he sold clothing for extra-large men. He insisted on wearing large sizes, so his pants drooped and the sleeves of his suit jackets hung over his knuckles. He was quite a sight. Bobby Bluntnose also had the opportunity. He admits he was in Bigstuff's office, firing his revolver at the time of the murder."

Dr. Quicksolve scratched the head of his retriever, Copper, as if to help the dog think.

Then he said, "Give me some more details."

"Bluntnose was in B.B.'s office at eight-forty-five, according to B.B.'s secretary. On the way out he told the secretary B.B. was on the phone and should not be disturbed. He also said he would be back soon.

"Bluntnose came back a few minutes later.

He was in the office just a couple minutes when the secretary heard two shots. A few seconds later Bluntnose ran out of the office with a gun in his hand and told the secretary to call the police. His story was that a woman shot Bigstuff through the window, and he shot at the assailant as she ran off. Bigstuff was killed with a .22 caliber bullet, and Bluntnose had a .38 with one shot fired. So it looks as if he's telling the truth," Lieutenant Rootumout said.

"There is a way he could have done it," Dr. Quicksolve said.

How?

Solution on page 329.

6

THOMAS P. STANWICK

EVEN THOSE UNACQUAINTED with Thomas P. Stanwick are often struck by his appearance. A lean and lanky young man, he stands six feet two inches tall. His long, thin face is complemented by a full head of brown hair and a droopy mustache. Though not husky in build, he is surprisingly strong and enjoys ruggedly good health.

His origins and early life are obscure. He is undeniably well educated, having graduated with high honors from Dartmouth College as a philosophy major and studied logic and history at Cambridge University for a year or two afterwards. He now lives alone (with a pet Labrador) in a bungalow in the New England town of Baskerville, not far from the city of Royston. He earns a living as a freelance editor of textbooks on  geometry and American history. Stanwick spends many of his evenings conversing with friends at the Royston Chess Club and elsewhere. When he has a hand in investigating and solving crimes, it is usually through his friend Inspector Matt Walker, a detective on the Royston police force. Stanwick is fascinated by puzzles and mysteries of all kinds, but his major interest in criminal cases is that of a logician. In that capacity, Walker would be the first to admit, he is frequently very useful.

Death in the Garage

INSPECTOR MATTHEW WALKER and Thomas P. Stanwick had barely begun their weekly game that Thursday evening at the chess club when Walker's beeper went off.

"There's been a suspicious death in Caterina Road," said Walker when he returned from the phone. "Probably a suicide. Care to come?"

"By all means. Some evenings aren't made for chess."

A quarter of an hour later, Walker and

Stanwick were in the garage of Walter McCarthy, a real estate broker. McCarthy was seated behind the wheel of his car, dead. The garage door was open, the car was silent, and the police were busily at work.

"The body was discovered by Mrs. McCarthy when she returned home on foot about six," reported Sergeant Hatch. "The car was running. Nearly overcome by exhaust fumes herself, she opened the garage door from the inside, switched off the car and called 9-1-1 from the kitchen. She's inside now."

"Cause of death established?" asked Walker.

"The medical examiner says the body shows signs of carbon monoxide asphyxiation. We did find these in the right jacket pocket, though."

Hatch handed Walker a plastic evidence bag containing a pill bottle. Walker gingerly removed the bottle, glanced at the label, and popped open the cap. The bottle was half full of large, pink lozenges.

"A prescription depressant," he remarked.

"Refilled only yesterday for one pill a day, and yet half the pills are gone. Could these have killed him?"

"No, they couldn't," responded Dr. Pillsbury, the owlish medical examiner, who now approached Walker. "If he took half the bottle, though, the dose would have knocked him out in about fifteen seconds."

"But why would he take the pills if he were about to asphyxiate himself anyway?" asked Stanwick. "Asphyxiation is painless."

Pillsbury shrugged. "It is. But he may have wanted to put himself under sooner, before he could lose his nerve. I've seen it before in suicides."

"Hatch," said Walker, turning to the sergeant, "what was found in the car?"

"Nothing unusual, sir. Registration, maps, ice scraper, a scarf, a bag of chips. A folder of house listings. In the trunk, some tools, a spare, jumper cables, a blanket."

"Has a suicide note turned up?"

"Not yet, sir. We're still checking the house."

"And how much gas was in the tank?" asked Stanwick.

"Oh, plenty, sir. More than enough."

"Thank you, sergeant," said Walker. "Please tell Mrs. McCarthy I'll see her soon.

"Yes, sir."

As Hatch strode off, Walker turned back to Stanwick. "Well, Tom, I'm afraid there's not much of special interest here. Whether or not we find a note, this looks to me like a straightforward suicide."

Stanwick shook his head solemnly. "I don't think so, Matt," he replied. "Though I can't be certain, I think this is a case of murder.

Why does Stanwick think McCarthy was murdered?

Solution on pages 329–330.

The Case of the Dubious Drowning

"A DROWNING AT DUNCOMB residence, 857 Whippoorwill Drive. Victim middle-aged woman. Ambulance and unit en route."

Inspector Matt Walker and Thomas P. Stanwick listened intently to the terse announcement on Walker's police radio. Whippoorwill Drive was only minutes away, so without a word, Walker, who was giving Stanwick a ride home, turned his car toward it.

The ambulance and a police car arrived just before them. Walker and Stanwick followed the commotion to the swimming pool, about 60 feet in back of the formidable Duncomb mansion. The emergency crew had just pulled Marjorie Duncomb from the pool and was trying to revive her. A moment later they hoisted her, still dripping in her swimsuit, onto a stretcher and rushed her to the ambulance.

"No life signs, sir," one medical technician said to Walker as he hurried past. Walker turned to the two police officers and a disheveled, graying man standing by the pool.

"Mr. Duncomb?" he asked, flashing his badge. "Did you call this in?"

"Yes," replied the disheveled man, still staring toward the departing ambulance. "I found

Marjorie face-down in the pool. The poor dear must have had a heart attack during her swim and drowned."

"Were you looking for her?"

"Yes. I knew she was late getting back from her swim. It was after three."

"Did she swim every day, then?"

"That's right. Even now, in October. It's getting chilly, though, so we were going to close up the pool for the season next week. Only next week!"

Stanwick glanced around. The pool was well maintained, but the furnishings were few: three lounge chairs and a small table. A pair of sandals lay beside one of the chairs, and a book and a pair of sunglasses lay on the table.

"Did your wife have a weak heart, Mr. Duncomb?" asked Stanwick.

"Just a bit of angina, but she took medication for it. Poor dear!"

"Matt," said Stanwick quietly, drawing Walker aside. "If Mrs. Duncomb cannot be revived, will an autopsy be required?"

"Of course."

"Well, I think you will find little or no water in her lungs. This is wrong. She didn't drown. She died elsewhere and was moved to the pool, which indicates murder. Until the autopsy results are in, I think you had better keep an eye on the husband."

Why does Stanwick suspect that Mrs. Duncomb was murdered?

Solution on page 330.

The Churchill Letter

"MRS. BRYANT! It's nice to see you again. Please come in."

Thomas P. Stanwick stood back from the door and waved his gray-haired visitor into his living room.

"I'm sorry to bother you again, Mr. Stanwick," said Ellen Bryant, as she settled herself onto the sofa, "but you were so helpful with my earlier difficulty that I hoped you might advise me on this one."

"Certainly, if I can," replied Stanwick. Striding to the sideboard, he began to prepare a tray of fresh tea. "What's the problem?"

"A few days ago," she said, "I was visited by Stephen Faybush, the nephew of a couple I know in my neighborhood. He specializes in unusual investments."

"Indeed?" said Stanwick. He brought the

tray over and poured two cups of Lapsang souchong. "Have you been looking for investment advice?"

"Well, I have a small nest egg that isn't earning much in the bank, and I may have mentioned this to my neighbors."

"And what sorts of investment does this Faybush promote?"

"Historical artifacts, mostly. Famous signatures and such. He says they consistently beat inflation as they rise in value over time."

"That's true—if they are genuine, that is." Stanwick settled himself near her on the sofa. "Do you by chance have such an item in your folder there?"

"Exactly, yes." Mrs. Bryant opened a manila folder she had been carrying and extracted a letter. "It's a Churchill," she said, as she handed it to Stanwick.

Stanwick held the document gingerly and gave a low whistle.

"A letter from Churchill's private secretary to a John McMasters," he murmured. "Not a name I recognize. Probably a constituent. 'Sir Winston very much appreciates the book you sent him' and so on. Dated in the mid-1950s. Cream-colored paper. Letterhead refers to Chartwell, Churchill's country home. The valuable bit is the handwritten inscription 'With warmest good wishes, Winston S. Churchill' along the bottom after the secretary's signature. Only about a year and a half later, he returned to power as Prime Minister."

"Stephen is urging me to buy it," said Mrs. Bryant. "He is letting me keep it and look it over this week."

Stanwick smiled faintly.

"My advice," he said, "is to have nothing more to do with Mr. Faybush. In fact, I think I'll place a call to the local constabulary about him. This letter is a fraud. May I suggest that you find a good mutual fund for your money?"

*How does Stanwick know the letter
is a fraud?*

Solution on page 330.

A Stamp of Suspicion

THOMAS P. STANWICK and Inspector Matthew Walker were chatting in the lounge of the Royston Chess Club after an arduous game.

"Any interesting cases on hand, Matt?" asked Stanwick, lighting his pipe.

Walker nodded. "A robbery case involving a stamp collector. What's driving me nuts is that I think the victim may be lying, but I can't prove it."

"Really?" Stanwick arched his eyebrows. "Please tell me about it."

"It happened, supposedly, three nights ago, in one of the mansions up on the Hill," Walker said. "The owner, Avery Manlich, says that he was awakened about 2 A.M. by a noise downstairs in his library. Grasping a baseball bat, he crept down the stairs and paused there to switch on the light to the foyer. He also called out 'Who's there?' in the direction of the library.

"To his astonishment, two men darted out of the library and ran out the front door into the night. By the time the shocked Manlich rushed to the open door, the men were gone. Only then did he go back to the library and find his safe cracked and at least ten trays of valuable stamps missing. "

"Just a moment," interrupted Stanwick. "While he was at the door, did he hear any car

doors slamming or an engine starting?"

"No, he didn't. The thieves escaped on foot."

"Did Manlich describe the thieves?"

"Nothing very helpful. He said the men were dressed only in black, skintight leotards, black gloves, and black ski masks. As they ran out, both had their arms full of several trays of stamps."

"And what did your investigation reveal?"

"The deadbolt lock on the front door had been sawed off, the other lock on that door had been picked, and the safe (a rather sophisticated one) had been expertly cracked.

No fingerprints or other physical evidence was left, and according to Manlich, nothing but the stamps was taken. The stamps were heavily insured, of course. Neither on the grounds nor in the surrounding area have we found any discarded ski masks or other traces of the thieves."

"And on what basis do you doubt Manlich's story?"

Walker made a wry face.

"Not much more than a gut feeling, I guess,"

he said. "I've dealt with collectors before, Tom. Though usually normal in all other respects, they tend to be fanatical when it comes to their collections. This guy Manlich, it seems to me, has been just a little too cool about this whole thing. Of course, it's nothing I could take to court."

"No, I suppose not," said Stanwick with a smile. "I think a more solid basis can be found, however, for your suspicions about Manlich. His story does contain a major flaw!"

What flaw did Stanwick detect in Manlich's story?

Solution on pages 330–331.

The Case of the Purloined Painting

THERE WERE TIMES, thought Thomas P. Stanwick, when you could never have a friendly conversation without an interruption. Especially if your friend was a police inspector and you were visiting his office when a robbery call came in.

The amateur logician and Inspector Walker pulled up in front of a large brick house in a wealthy neighborhood in Royston and were quickly shown into the living room. A valuable painting had been stolen from the wall. The thief had apparently broken the glass in a nearby patio door, let himself in, and left by the same route. An obviously shaken maid was sitting in a large armchair when Stanwick and Walker entered.

"She discovered the theft and called it in, sir," a uniformed officer told Walker. "The couple who live here are out of town this week."

"What happened?" Walker asked the maid.

"I didn't hear a thing," she replied. "I had been working in the kitchen and was on my way to my room. When I passed the living room, I noticed that the painting was gone and that the glass in the patio door was broken. I called the police right away."

Stanwick carefully opened the patio door and walked out onto the concrete patio, stepping gingerly around the long shards of broken glass there as well as around any possible footmarks. He observed faint smudges of mud under the glass.

"How long had the painting hung in here?" he asked as he came back in.

"About two years, I guess," answered the maid.

Stanwick sat down in a comfortable armchair, crossed his legs, and turned to Walker.

"Well, Matt," he said, "I think you may want to ask this lady some more questions. This job involved inside help!"

Why is Stanwick sure that inside help was involved?

Solution on page 331.

The Stockbroker's Last Morning

SHORTLY AFTER NINE one morning, Inspector Walker's car pulled up in front of a large office building in downtown Royston. With Walker was Thomas P. Stanwick, who had been visiting with Walker at headquarters when the call reporting the sudden death of Charles Steinberg came in.

Stanwick and Walker hurried to Steinberg's seventh-floor office suite, from which he had run a prosperous stock brokerage firm. Passing through the carpeted reception area, they entered Steinberg's spacious office.

Steinberg's body was slumped in an easy chair near a small, circular table in the center of the room. His tie and collar were loose. He had been dead for less than an hour, and showed no

sign of bleeding. On a small table by the wall, a typewriter contained a typed note, which Stanwick read aloud.

I see no further purpose to my life and have therefore decided to end it. I hope my family, friends, and associates will not blame themselves.
Goodbye.

Walker turned to the man in his early 30's who was standing near the office door. Jon Golding was a vice president of the firm.

"What can you tell us, Mr. Golding?"

Golding coughed nervously.

"I entered Mr. Steinberg's office earlier this morning to see him on urgent business. He was sitting in the easy chair with a cup of coffee in his hand. As soon as he saw me, he hastily drank it down. The cup had no sooner left his lips than he was seized with terrible convulsions. A few seconds later he was dead. I was horrified and ran out to the receptionist's desk, where I phoned for help. No one was allowed into the office until you arrived."

"Did you see the note in the typewriter?"

"No, sir, I did not."

"Thank you." Walker went over to Steinberg's body and searched his pockets. In the right jacket pocket he found a small glass vial, which he sniffed. "This probably contained the poison."

Stanwick sniffed it and, taking out his handkerchief, picked up the emptied coffee cup from its saucer on the table and sniffed it also.

"I can detect a whiff of it here, too," he said.

Stanwick put down the coffee cup and faced Golding.

"Mr. Golding," he asked, "did Mr. Steinberg usually have his coffee in that chair?"

"Yes, sir, he drank his coffee and read the paper in that chair every morning about this time."

Stanwick pointed to a newspaper folded neatly on the table. "Did you put that there?"

Golding flushed slightly. "It was there when I came in. He wasn't reading it."

Stanwick abruptly left the office and walked to the desk of the young receptionist.

"What can you tell us, Miss Gwynne?"

"Why, little enough, I'm afraid. I heard some typing in Mr. Steinberg's office, and then Mr. Golding came out of his own office to pick up some documents for Mr. Steinberg. He went into Mr. Steinberg's office and a few moments later came rushing wildly out here and phoned for help."

"What documents did he want to show Mr. Steinberg?"

"Why, some draft pages of our weekly newsletter. He dropped them on the floor as he came back out."

Reentering Steinberg's office, Stanwick put another question to Golding. "I see there is a door between your office and this. Why didn't you use that when you came in to see him?"

"Miss Gwynne, our receptionist, had the

newsletter pages I wanted to show him," Golding answered.

Stanwick quietly drew Walker aside.

"Golding is lying, Matt," he said. "This isn't suicide, but murder!"

How does Stanwick know Golding is lying?

Solution on pages 331–332.

Death of a Kingpin

THOMAS P. STANWICK'S visit that day to Inspector Walker's office was particularly well timed. Walker was just leaving to visit the scene of the murder of Aaron Griffith of Hubbard Drive, a moneyed neighborhood, and he invited the amateur logician to join him.

"Frankly, I'm not surprised Griffith took a bullet," remarked Walker during the drive. "Two, actually. He was a drug kingpin, and we'd been watching him for some time. He worked from an upstairs office in his home with a bodyguard outside the door. Not much of a retinue for someone in his position."

"It sounds like the bodyguard had his limitations," Stanwick observed.

Walker grunted. "Well, he paid the price for them. He was gunned down too. Griffith had enough life left after being shot to call us. Listen to this."

Walker inserted a cassette tape into his tape deck and pressed a button. A moment later a desperate voice filled the car.

"This is Griffith...I've been shot...It was Ren...Ren...."

"Too bad he couldn't get out the rest of the name," said Walker as he stopped the tape. "His appointment book showed that he saw a delegation of three men this morning: Albert Wrenville, Barry Renfeld, and Carl Rennecker."

"Ren, Ren, and Ren," murmured Stanwick. "At least phonetically. Any other visitors that we know of?"

"Only his sister from across town. Flora. Well, here we are."

Two minutes later, Walker and Stanwick were standing by the body of the guard outside the door to Griffith's office. The door was at the end of a long hardwood hallway. Five feet down from the guard, a wall section was slid back to

reveal a passage within the wall. Walker looked inside it and whistled softly.

"A hidden passage!" he exclaimed. "You don't often see one of these. But I suppose Griffith wanted an escape route." He and Stanwick stepped into the carpeted, paneled

195

office of the victim, where Sergeant Hatch joined them.

"The guard was shot at close range, sir," he reported to Walker. "Two to three feet. Doc Pillsbury says he was killed first. Griffith appears to have been shot from the doorway. It's about 20 feet from there to the desk."

The desk, a massive creation of oak, stood in the center of the room facing the doorway. Slumped over the desk in his own blood lay the kingpin, his right hand clutching the telephone. The still-lit computer console, the gold pen set, several folders, and the appointment diary were spattered with blood as well. At the desk and elsewhere in the room, the investigative team was working quietly and efficiently.

"Shot in the chest and the throat, to use layman's terms," Pillsbury, the medical examiner, noted tersely. "Amazed he could still talk, but it's not impossible."

"Who were the Rens, anyway?" Stanwick suddenly asked Walker.

"More dirtbags. Wrenville had drug connections in South America and had just come up from there. This was his first meeting with Griffith. Renfeld belongs to one of the big drug 'families'; he's done business with Griffith a couple of times before. Rennecker, who used to be Griffith's personal assistant, is his affiliate (so to speak) in the western part of the state. I looked them up on the police network before heading over here."

"And his sister—was she here before the Rens?"

"Yes, at 8:30. The Rens were here at 10. It looks like one of the Rens, who came in separate cars, either lingered behind or returned alone. They apparently have no common interest in Griffith's death."

"In that case, one or two at least plausible deductions can be made," said Stanwick. "For one, it was indeed one of the Rens. For another, I think I can name which one it was."

Who murdered Griffith?

Solution on page 332.

The Bracken Park Incident

"SHE SAYS SHE NEVER saw who attacked her," said Inspector Walker. "I've just come from the hospital. She's still pretty groggy, though, and may remember more later."

The inspector and Thomas P. Stanwick, the amateur logician, were striding briskly that crisp November morning through the streets of Royston toward Bracken Park. Earlier that morning, Alison Vaneer, a beautician in her early 30's, had been hit on the head and robbed while jogging through the park.

"When was she found?" asked Stanwick.

"About 8:30, by another jogger, just where the path passes a clump of trees. She was attacked a little after 7:00, just at daybreak. The money belt she wore around her stomach had been taken, and she was suffering from a concussion. For such chilly weather, she wasn't wearing much: a T-shirt, a tennis skirt, jacket with a reflector, a Harvard sweatshirt. And a baseball cap."

"Ah, a sedentary fellow like you wouldn't appreciate how warm some exercise can keep one," remarked Stanwick wryly.

Walker snorted. "And you would?"

They stopped by a news kiosk several yards from the south gate to the park.

"She entered the park through here," Walker said. "It's her usual route." With a flash of his badge, Walker introduced himself to the news-dealer, Oscar Kramer.

"Did you see a woman jogger go into the park this morning?" he asked.

"A few, actually," Kramer answered. "Which one?"

"The one with the Harvard sweatshirt," said Stanwick.

"Oh, yeah. Around seven, just as I was start-ing to open up. She's gone by every morning for the last couple of weeks, just like clockwork. Why?"

"She was attacked and robbed in the park," replied Walker impassively. "Did you see any suspicious persons enter or leave the park this way this morning?"

Kramer shook his head. "No, sir."

"Thank you," said Walker. "Sergeant Hatch will be along shortly to take your statement." He and Stanwick resumed their walk.

"Hatch is still at the crime scene," Walker told Stanwick as they entered the park. "It's about 50 yards up this way."

"I suggest he question Kramer carefully," said Stanwick with a frown. "That newsdealer could easily enough have anticipated Miss Vaneer's time and route, and lain in wait for her. He also knows more about this crime than he told us—no doubt of that!"

Why does Stanwick suspect the newsdealer of the crime?

Solution on pages 332–333.

The Adventure of the Negative Clue

NOT EVEN THE UNUSUAL heat of that late spring day could dissuade Thomas P. Stanwick from driving into the city. The amateur logician had learned that one of Royston's most select book dealers was holding a sale of rare folios at two in the afternoon. His bibliophilic instincts aroused, Stanwick was braving the heat and the downtown traffic he detested when the police radio in his car reported a murder nearby.

A middle-aged man had been stabbed to death in Hardee's Hardware Store three blocks away. Squad cars were told to watch for a white male of five feet, ten inches, 160 pounds, about 22 years old, with black hair and a pencil mustache, wearing a white T-shirt, a leather jacket, and blue jeans.

Stanwick wrestled with his competing interests for two seconds and then turned toward the hardware store. Parking his car down the block, he walked through a curious throng and, with a flash of his police pass, entered the shop.

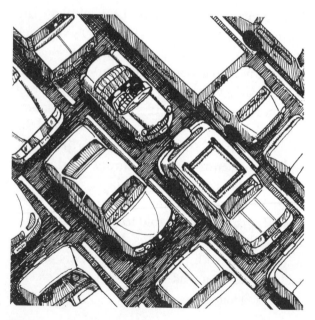

Inspector Walker arched his sandy eyebrows in surprise as he caught sight of his friend.

"Hello, Matt," said Stanwick. "I heard the bulletin on the radio and thought I'd stop by for a look."

"Glad to see you, Tom." Walker nodded to a dead body crumpled on the floor in front of the sales counter. "There's what there is to look at."

The victim was a dark-haired man in his middle 40's. He lay face up. The handle of a knife protruded from his ribs, and a circle of blood had soaked through his blue suit.

"His wallet is missing," Walker reported drily, "as is a briefcase the sales clerk said he was carrying when he came in. From other papers in his pockets, we've identified him as Hubert French, an accounting executive from Helston."

"Did the clerk see it happen?" asked Stanwick, glancing at a thin, balding man lurking behind the counter.

"No. He says French came in to pick up a

special wrench he had ordered. A guy fitting the bulletin description came in just a few seconds later. The clerk went to the back to get the wrench. While there, he heard sounds of a scuffle and a cry from here. He rushed in and found French dead and the other fellow gone."

Stanwick fingered the tip of his mustache. "Any prints on the weapon?"

Walker shook his head. "No. The clerk says our suspect wore gloves."

Just then the outer door opened, and two policemen entered with a manacled man closely fitting the description given on the radio.

"Inspector, this is T.A. Orrison," said the older officer. "We found him four blocks away, walking briskly down Jefferson. Says he was on his way home after slicing fish in the back of Radford's Fish Mart all morning. He fits the description, though, so we picked him up."

Walker looked coldly at Orrison, who was wearing green sunglasses.

"What do you know about this, Mr. Orrison?"

he demanded, pointing at the corpse.

"Nothing," Orrison replied angrily. "I was at work all morning. I haven't been in this place for at least three weeks."

"How long have you worked at Radford's?"

"Two months now, part-time. I work from seven to noon, six days a week. I put in some overtime today and was just on the way home when I was grabbed by these two guys in a squad car and brought here."

A mild, metallic odor suffused the small shop. Stanwick wandered to a window, opened it partway, and gazed idly out. Walker continued his questions.

"You implied that you visited this shop a few weeks ago. Why?"

"I dunno. I had to get nails or tape or something."

"Why did you work late today?"

"We got a big catch in this morning, and I was the only one there."

Walker signaled to the uniformed officers.

"All right, that's enough for here. Take him to the station for more questioning."

Once the others had left, Stanwick rejoined the inspector.

"When you get back, Matt," he said, "you may as well book him for the murder. He's your man."

Walker turned to him in astonishment. "What makes you so sure? I'll admit he's on shaky ground, but I don't see any conclusive clue."

Stanwick smiled.

"In a way, there isn't one," he replied. "What's really significant in this case is what you could call a negative clue—the one that isn't here!"

What is the negative clue?

Solution on page 333.

Table of Death

JUST AS INSPECTOR WALKER'S hand was hovering over a bishop, his beeper alarm sounded. With an impatient sigh, he pushed back his chair and stood up. Across the chessboard, Thomas P. Stanwick chuckled softly.

"Saved by the beep!" he exclaimed.

"Don't be so sure of that!" Walker retorted as he started toward the Royston Chess Club lobby and a telephone. One minute later, he was back.

"Gotta go," he said hurriedly. "Two bodies in an apartment. Want to come?"

"Certainly."

Twenty minutes later, Stanwick and Walker were in a seedy, third-floor apartment downtown. The place consisted of a bedroom and a small kitchen off a sparsely furnished sitting room. In the center of the sitting room stood a square wooden table supporting a half-full pitcher of purple liquid, two drained glasses, several incense candles, a few small piles of powder, and a handwritten note with two signatures.

On the floor by the table lay the bodies of two middle-aged men, each by an overturned wooden chair. Sergeant Hatch and the crime scene unit were already at work when Walker and Stanwick arrived.

"The fellow in the undershirt is George Barnes, the tenant here," Hatch reported. "The one in the suit is Theo Hunter, an insurance salesman. We've checked their pockets. The candles and drugs are similar to those used in some cult out West. The note, signed by both, is a suicide pact. It's pretty weird, sir."

"Will that word appear on your report, sergeant?" said Walker with a wry half-smile. "Let's see what was in their pockets."

"This way, sir." Hatch led them to a side table. "Barnes had these tissues and keys, and this comb and wallet. The rest is Hunter's. Handkerchief, keys, penknife, business cards, wallet, comb, a folded gas receipt from earlier today, a folded insurance application from last week."

"Hmm." Walker turned to the approaching medical examiner. "Any verdict, Doc?"

"Not yet, of course," replied Dr. Pillsbury peevishly. "You must await the autopsy. The external symptoms, though, are of a swift-acting poison."

Walker glanced at Stanwick. "You've been awfully quiet, Tom."

Stanwick, who had been leaning against the wall and staring at the table, snapped out of his reverie.

"It's a small room and a busy investigation," he said. "Just trying to stay out of the way. I suggest that you check the signatures on that note carefully, though."

"Oh?" Walker arched his sandy eyebrows. "That's routine, of course, but why do you say that?"

"I think one of the signatures is forged. This looks to me like a murder-suicide. One poisoned the other and then made it look like a double suicide. And I can tell you which was the murderer."

Which was the murderer? How does Stanwick know?

Solution on page 333.

7
INSPECTOR FORSOOTH

THE MYSTERIES in this section are like no others you've ever tried. For starters, they've all been tested live in an AOL "auditorium" in front of hundreds of cybersleuths. These intrepid sleuths read the mystery text and then fired literally thousands of questions at Inspector Forsooth. The questions and answers that accompany each mystery are taken directly from these online solving sessions.

Each mystery contains a mosaic of clues that the sleuth—that's you—must piece together to divine the solution. You'll be aided by the Q&A session, which flushes out each and every tiny clue hidden in the test. You can read all the answers or test yourself by reading only a few. It's all up to you.

Inspector Forsooth

Halloween Horror

BEING A GHOST for Halloween is one thing. Becoming a ghost is another. But that's what happened to one teenage girl on this scariest of Halloweens.

The trick-or-treating part of the evening went about as expected, with house after house trembling as her wispy figure made its way up the front steps. The ghost lived in a town where folks took their costumes seriously, and people were especially generous to inspired creations. By the time the night was through, she had amassed enough goodies to last her until Thanksgiving. But she didn't last even one day, thanks to a fatal choice of late-night snack.

In the ghost's possession at the time of her death was a half-eaten Butterfinger bar, which was immediately sent to the toxicology lab.

The results showed that the candy bar had been laced with rat poison: It must have been doctored and rewrapped, but the ghost never noticed it. But even if the question of how she died could be resolved, it wasn't at all clear who might have wanted her out of the way.

In real life, the ghost was in junior high school. She was a good student, seemingly without an enemy in the world. She was also a shoo-in to make the cheerleading squad for the upcoming basketball season. And with that small fact, a motive began to take shape. The problem was that the candy bar could have come from virtually anybody along her Halloween route.

The ghost's route on her final Halloween journey was painstakingly retraced, and some curious facts turned up: For one, she had been trick-or-treating with a group of friends until fairly late in the evening, and all were pretty sure that the ghost hadn't picked up any Butterfinger bars during their escapades. But after leaving her friends, she had gone to four houses in a final circle near her own home. And of those four families, three of them had a daughter who was vying for the same cheerleading squad. The families in question were the Ackmans, the Bartosavages, and the Claxtons, whom the ghost visited in that order. Her final stop came at Old Lady MacDonald's house up on the hill; the old lady was a widow, and her kids had all grown up and moved away.

The interviews with these residents left the police no closer than they had been at first. Everyone professed outrage at the heinous Halloween crime that had shaken the neighborhood. Each said that the ghost was one of the last trick-or-treaters they had that night (the earlier part of the evening having been taken up with younger kids), and each of them fiercely denied an attempt to poison for the sake of cheerleading—although they had all heard stories about such overzealous parents.

Not wanting to miss any detail, the police

compiled records of how everyone was disguised that night. It turned out that Mr. Ackman had greeted his arrivals in his customary devil suit. Mrs. Bartosavage had greeted her callers in a light-up skeleton costume whose bones glowed in the dark. Mr. Claxton had devised a special outfit in which a woman's mask, etc., were placed on his back, so that he approached his guests facing backwards! When he turned around, the effect was creepy indeed. And Old Lady MacDonald, who was approaching 80 years of age, rose to the occasion by simply taking out her dentures and painting her face green. That, coupled with a mole or two on her cheek, made her the scariest witch of the night.

Of these four houses, only two—the Ackmans and the Bartosavages—had any Butterfinger bars remaining from Halloween. The ones they had left over were tested for rat poison, but those tests all came back negative. As for the Claxtons, they claimed to have treated visitors with many other items—M&Ms, Hershey's, and Mars bars, among others. As for Mrs. MacDonald, she was known to be the least generous of all the neighborhood stops, and she only had licorice and saltwater taffy, which some trick-or-treaters suspected had been left over from the previous year!

One question that puzzled the investigators was that there had been two other girls who paraded through the neighborhood just before the ghost came. The first had been dressed as Mary Poppins. The second—wouldn't you know it—came dressed as a cheerleader. And both of them were trying out for the cheerleading team in real life. The existence of these two girls threw a monkey wrench into the entire investigation, because it wasn't clear whether the ghost had been singled out, or whether the killer would have been happy to knock anyone off just to create one more space on the squad.

However, Inspector Forsooth thought it extremely likely that the ghost had in fact been singled out of the crowd. Acting on that assumption, he was able to identify the perptrator.

1) *Who killed the ghost?*

2) *How could the killer feel confident that no one other than the intended victim would be killed by the poison?*

3) *How did the killer's choice of costume play a role?*

INSPECTOR FORSOOTH ANSWERS YOUR QUESTIONS

Q1–Was the victim still wearing her costume when she died?

No, she was not wearing her costume.

Q2–How did the killer know who the ghost was?

The killer found out through the grapevine, meaning that there was discussion about who was dressing up as what, so the ghost's identity was known in advance.

Q3–Was there anyone else dressed as a ghost that night?

Not in that neighborhood, no.

Q4–How did they know she would pick that particular Butterfinger bar?

It was the only Butterfinger bar there!

Q5–Did any of the people in the suspect houses know that the victim was coming by?

No. They had no idea who was coming until they got there.

Q6–Does the fact that the ghost left her friends to go alone have any significance?

Yes, it is quite significant. Had the ghost not

gone out alone, there could never have been any assurance that she would pick up the tainted bar.

Q7–Was it important that the ghost was one of the last trick-or-treaters?

It sure was.

Q8–Did the ghost choose her own candy, or was it handed to her?

Great question. The ghost chose her own candy.

Q9–Were Butterfingers the victim's favorite candy bar?

No, they weren't necessarily her favorite, but they were certainly preferable to other choices.

Q10–So the widow, who had bad candy, wanted the cheerleader dead, and she put a good candy in with the bad candy?

I didn't say that! What motive could she possibly have had?

Q11–What do Mrs. MacDonald's teeth have to do with it?

Well, remember that the killer wasn't taking any chances that the poisoned Butterfinger bar might end up in the wrong hands—or mouth.

Q12–Did the Mary Poppins carry an umbrella?

Sure did. And you're on the right track—but it looks as though you have to dig a little deeper.

Can you solve the mystery?

Solution on pages 334–335.

The Prints of Lightness

AFTER IT WAS ALL OVER, the workmen outside Oscar Delahanty's home could barely comprehend the irony of what had just taken place. The men had arrived promptly at 8:30 one summer morning to install a roadside fire hydrant some fifty feet or so from Delahanty's front walkway. Barely an hour into their job, well before the new hydrant was operational, they saw smoke billowing out of a first-floor window. They contacted their buddies at the fire department, who got down as quickly as they could. However, by the time the firefighters arrived, Delahanty's small but historic home had already sustained significant damage. And that wasn't all.

When the firemen on the scene trudged upstairs to Delahanty's bedroom, they found him lying in bed, quite dead. He was still dressed in his blue silk pajamas, so clearly he hadn't enjoyed much of this sultry summer morning. The fire itself hadn't reached the upstairs, but there was plenty of smoke all around. The firemen noticed that the window

in his bedroom, which looked out onto the road, was firmly shut.

The blaze had apparently started near the back door, which was part of the "newer" section of the house. By the looks of things, the hardwood floors in that area, including the back staircase, had just been refinished, but they had been almost completely torched by the blaze. Officials couldn't be certain just what had been used to ignite the fire, but they doubted that it had started by accident.

The fire chief found that everything in the house seemed to be in compliance with local regulations. However, he couldn't help but note that older houses were notoriously poor fire risks, and an alarm system directly wired into the fire department would have saved time and prevented some of the damage they were witnessing. Implicit in his remark was that a better system might have saved Delahanty's life.

The next step was to alert Delahanty's employees at The Clip Joint, the hair salon he had owned and operated for just over six years. When the authorities got there, they could see that it was a busy morning, rendered all the busier by the boss's no-show. The three stylists on the job were Gigi LaCroix, Stan Norton, and Mitchell Quinn, each of whom had worked for Delahanty since the salon opened. When told that their boss had died of asphyxia, all three were momentarily speechless. After this stunned silence was over, Quinn said he would phone the boss's other appointments and officially cancel them. Gigi LaCroix had already placed a call to Delahanty's home, but had gotten only his answering machine. She asked if the house was damaged in the fire, and expressed relief that it could probably be rebuilt. As for Stan Norton, he had apparently been planning on visiting the boss's home himself to see what was wrong, but now he did not have to.

The investigators took careful note of these various reactions, but it wasn't until 24 hours had elapsed that a possible motive appeared. A woman named Hilda Graylock came forward to say that Delahanty had offered her a job as a stylist with his salon. He indicated to her that he was planning on letting one of his staff go, but she didn't know which one. To make matters even more interesting, not long after Graylock gave her testimony, another woman appeared at the police station and gave the exact same story! These tidbits certainly changed the complexion of things, and, upon consultation with the medical examiner, police now concluded definitively that Delahanty had been murdered.

Upon returning to the salon, the authorities picked up some more information about what happened that morning. Mitchell Quinn testified that he had opened up the salon at 8:00 A.M. It was The Clip Joint's policy to rotate the responsibility for the 8:00 shift; the rest of the staff would come in later in the morning, well in time for the lunchtime crunch. The salon stayed open until 8:30 at night, and the bulk of its business was conducted at lunchtime and during the evening hours.

As it happened, everyone had worked late the night before Delahanty's death. LaCroix and Norton had gone out for a drink and a bite to eat afterwards; they were joined by a couple from the massage studio located right next to The Clip Joint. That little gathering didn't break up until about midnight, whereupon everybody went home. As for the next morning, LaCroix had come in about 9:30, while Norton had arrived at a couple of minutes past ten, something of an annoyance to his 10:00 appointment.

A revisiting of the crime scene offered a couple of important details. Ordinarily, the back door to Delahanty's home would have been locked with a dead bolt, which was of course activated from the inside. But whoever had done the floorwork had exited that way, and was unable to lock the door on the way out! So that explained how the killer could have entered the home without forced entry and without the workmen seeing him or her. Because of the layout of the house, it would have been quite easy for someone to have entered the back way without being spotted.

Upon hearing this crucial piece of information, Hilda Graylock lamented Delahanty's bad luck. He had evidently sought permission from the town clerk's office for several months to get the floors redone. (Because much of the house dated back to the early 18th century, it had attained landmark status, so he couldn't do much without the town's approval.) However, the "newer" wing, although still a century old, did not have quite the same restrictions, so the work was approved, as long as the wood was stained in a manner consistent with the rest of the woodwork. And just a day after the work was complete, Delahanty was dead.

Before the authorities could get around to identifying the murderer, they received more than they could possibly have hoped for—a confession. That's right, one of Delahanty's employees admitted to having killed the boss.

Ordinarily the investigation might have ended right then and there, but in this case police truly got too much of a good thing. Later that same day, another Clip Joint employee admitted to having killed Delahanty! Neither confession could be readily dismissed. In fact, both people took lie detector tests, and they each passed with flying colors.

The bad news was that some important evidence had been destroyed. The good news was that the coroner's report turned out to invalidate one of the two confessions. Even without seeing that report, do you know who the real murderer was? Well, it's not easy, and a couple of issues will have to be resolved in the question-and-answer session that follows. But here are the questions you must answer:

1) Who killed Oscar Delahanty?

2) *Who wrongly confessed to the crime?*

3) *How did the coroner's report help identify the killer?*

4) *What was the "evidence" that was destroyed?*

INSPECTOR FORSOOTH ANSWERS YOUR QUESTIONS

Q1–Could Gigi or Stan have killed him the prior night?

No. The folks at the massage studio could attest to their whereabouts all night.

Q2–Why is it important that Delahanty lived in a landmark house?

Because it wouldn't have been possible for him to have central air conditioning. The fact that his bedroom window was closed suggests that there was no room air conditioner.

Q3–Since more than one person was being hired, does that mean that more than one person was being fired?

It certainly looks that way.

Q4–Did the floor refinishers leave the night before? If so, why didn't Delahanty check to make sure the doors were locked before going to bed?

The workmen had in fact left the night before, but they had essentially "painted in" the area near the back door, so Delahanty couldn't have gone into that area (to lock the door) without ruining the new finish.

Q5–Why was Gigi so concerned about the house?

Perhaps she had a sentimental streak, and didn't really like the idea of such a nice home being destroyed.

Q6–When the police said that the victim had been "asphyxiated," does that mean that he died of smoke inhalation?

Not necessarily. "Asphyxiation" technically refers to any situation where breathing is impaired, whether arising from smoke inhalation, strangulation, or whatever.

Q7–Did the house's landmark status mean that it couldn't have smoke alarms?

Not at all. In fact, it was even more important for Delahanty to have smoke alarms, precisely because antique houses are extremely flammable. And the fire chief would certainly have noticed had Delahanty's smoke alarms been absent or defective.

Q8–Why was a hydrant being installed at that particular location?

Pure chance. Presumably the town had simply decided that it needed more hydrants, and noted that there wasn't one close enough to Oscar and his neighbors. (On a personal note, Inspector Forsooth returned home one evening to find a fire hydrant installed on the road alongside his own house. It does happen!)

Q9–Did the work on the hydrant begin that day or earlier?

Great question. The answer is that the work began that very morning.

Q10–If it was a sultry morning, why were Oscar's windows closed?

Another excellent question. We can assume that Delahanty wouldn't have been able to get to sleep that night had his windows been closed.

Q11–Had the floor fully dried?

Given what we know about the weather, etc., it seems unlikely that the finish would have been perfectly dry. Some polyurethane finishes can take a full 24 hours to dry.

Q12—How many workmen does it take to install a fire hydrant?

No light bulb jokes, please. The answer is that it takes several people to do the job, primarily because they have to jackhammer through the pavement to get to the pipes.

Can you solve the mystery?

Solution on pages 335–337.

The Valentine's Day Massacre

IT WAS ONLY AFTER Rudy Marcus was killed that his community got a full taste of what his life was really like. Marcus seemed like your average, everyday, straight-laced, white-collar type. A CPA by training, he worked at the Ernst Brothers accounting firm, and by all indications had done quite well for himself.

He had the usual trappings—a nice car and a well-groomed house in the suburbs—all in keeping with his solid-citizen image. But there wasn't much flair to Rudy. Businesswise, Rudy's customers didn't hire him because of his imagination; they hired him for the decimal-point precision with which he approached life. At home, there hadn't been a Mrs. Marcus on the scene for several years. Most

people figured she had simply gotten bored.

However, within days of the discovery of Rudy's body, the entire picture changed. One of his neighbors, a Mrs. Cecily Wheelock, revealed that Rudy Marcus was in fact a closet Romeo, a prim accountant by day but a free-wheeling bon vivant by night. He was having dalliances with no fewer than three women at the time of his death, each one claiming to be Rudy's real girlfriend. Those three became the focus of an extensive murder investigation.

Fittingly, Rudy had been killed on Valentine's Day, and the murder scene was consistent with a classic crime of passion. Rudy's body lay on the kitchen floor with a knife in his back. The murder weapon was one of his own kitchen knives, which had been taken from its usual resting place on the magnetic rack. It appeared that someone had stabbed Rudy the Romeo when his back was turned. From the absence of a struggle, it was assumed that Rudy knew whoever had murdered him.

The first of Rudy's mistresses to emerge was Cornelia Devane, who worked at the Estée Lauder counter at the nearby Bloomingdale's. Ms. Devane said she had been seeing Rudy for over a year, and was shocked to find out that there could have been other women in his life. But as she reflected on their relationship, she realized that his availability was sporadic. She had always chalked his busy schedule up to work-related matters, but now she knew better.

Then there was Daphne Nagelson, who had met Rudy the old-fashioned way—as a tax client. She said she was absolutely convinced that Rudy loved her the most, and to prove it she brought out an emerald brooch he had given her for Valentine's Day. Rudy had bought the brooch while in South America a few months before.

The third of Rudy's girlfriends was Mary Stahl, the only one of the three who was married. She also happened to be a city council-woman, a highly visible role. Yet no one around her knew of her relationship with Rudy. One interesting aspect of the case, which Stahl shed light on, was that Rudy had been in California on a business trip for several days prior to his murder. Originally he was supposed to have returned on the 12th, but his client needed more help than he had planned, so he didn't return until the 13th—just one day before he was killed.

Some of the investigators wrinkled their eyebrows upon hearing that little nugget. Apparently they figured that their dead little Casanova might have had something going in other ports as well, but that was never substantiated. Mary Stahl confirmed that Rudy had been thinking about her during his trip, as she brought out a gold necklace he had bought for her while he was away.

It turned out that Rudy had prevailed upon Cornelia Devane to visit his house periodically while he was gone. Her main task was to water the plants, but he also wanted her to turn some lights on and off to thwart any potential burglars, and even to watch TV to give the house a "lived-in" look. Devane said she had done that same routine many times in the past, and expressed some feeling that she was being taken for granted. Rudy didn't call her while he was gone. However, he had unexpectedly stopped by her workplace on Valentine's Day to give her a present—a red silk scarf.

Daphne Nagelson told the police that she and Rudy had gone out to see the movie Bed of Roses the night before his death, and she produced the ticket stubs to prove it. Cecily Wheelock, the snoopy neighbor, said that Daphne had stopped by Rudy's house earlier on the 13th, and she didn't deny it. But she did deny having gone inside, saying that she just stopped by to drop off her Valentine present for Rudy. Mrs. Wheelock confirmed that Daphne had a little smile on her face when she left the house.

According to the "rotation" that seemed to

be developing, that left Mary Stahl as Rudy's companion on the fateful night of February 14th, and, sure enough, she admitted that they, too, had gone to see a movie. When pressed as to the title, she stammered Dead Man Walking, not liking the irony of the title one bit. The movie was her treat, so she also had ticket stubs to present, which indicated to the authorities that Rudy was still alive until at least 9:30 P.M., when the movie ended. The coroner had already estimated the time of death as being between 8:00 P.M. and 11:00 P.M., based on the preliminary examination of such factors as rigor mortis and eye fluids. So Rudy clearly didn't live very long after the movie. Stahl also admitted that she left a message on Rudy's answering machine the night before he came home. The police located that very message on the machine.

Just when it appeared that the investigation was at a standstill, Inspector Forsooth noted that based solely on the evidence they already had, there was strong reason to believe that one particular woman in Rudy's life had found out about at least one of the others. When the authorities went back to confront that woman, a confession resulted. Your job is to figure out who confessed.

1) Who killed Rudy Marcus?

2) Rudy's personality played a role in his demise, in two distinctly different ways. Name them.

3) The testimony of two particular people would prove very helpful in bringing the guilty party to justice. Which two?

INSPECTOR FORSOOTH ANSWERS YOUR QUESTIONS

Q1–Is it proven that Mary and Rudy stayed for the whole movie?

They could have left early, but I believe they stayed for the whole thing.

Q2–Since Cornelia was housesitting for Rudy, did she intercept Mary's message on the answering machine?

We have to assume that if Cornelia was in the house, she heard the message, because he had an answering machine, not voice mail.

Q3–Did the gifts have anything to do with the murder?

They sure did, but not in the way you might think.

Q4–Which of the presents Rudy gave was the most valuable?

The emerald brooch was the most valuable, followed by the gold necklace. The red silk scarf was a distant third.

Q5–Was there any perfume scent noticed around the body?

There was a vague scent of perfume around the house, but it wasn't concentrated around the body. Sorry!

Q6–Did the police talk to Mary Stahl's husband?

No, they didn't. Actually, one of the questions asks for two witnesses who might be helpful. I can tell you right now that only one of them is named in the text, so Mr. Stahl is a good guess for the other. Alas, he's not the one.

Q7–How do you know that Daphne only went in the vestibule?

We have to take her word on that. Besides, she was only there a second or two, as Cecily Wheelock could confirm.

Q8–What was Daphne's gift? Was Rudy home when she delivered it?

I don't know what Daphne's gift was, and it really doesn't matter. But I can say that Rudy wasn't home when she delivered it. And his absence turns out to be extremely important in reaching the solution.

Q9–Where in the United States did the murder take place?

Believe it or not, it doesn't really matter. But we can assume from the language in the text that it took place outside of California, and that is important!

Q10–Is the fact that Rudy is an accountant significant?

Yes. He made a living out of reducing people's taxes, including his own. Income tax, state tax, sales tax—he hated them all. And that, believe it or not, is a big clue.

Q11–Was Cornelia angry at Rudy for not calling her while he was away?

Perhaps, but his failure to do so is good for her in a different sense, which is explained in the solution.

Q12–Where was Rudy when the package was delivered?

Rudy was not home when a particular package was delivered. (I hope that's not misleading!)

Can you solve the mystery?

Solution on pages 337–338.

Where There's a Will . . .

MARION WEBSTER was one of the most eccentric people ever to walk the planet. To him, communication was a game, to be played for personal amusement and nothing else. And when he died, everyone else was left to explain exactly what had happened. It wasn't easy.

The occasion was the 35th birthday party of Webster's eldest daughter, Laura. Every one of his six children was able to make it home for the late-September festivities. Webster had three sons—Eugene, Herbert, and Biff—and three daughters—Laura, Gwen, and Dorothy. All were grown up, but none as yet had started families of their own, a fact that displeased Webster tremendously. As the family patriarch and himself a retired widower, he felt it was his role to push his children in every imaginable way, even if the results didn't always match his expectations. Unfortunately, he used his own will to reward or penalize his children's efforts. It was a fatal mistake.

Instead of simply dividing his estate equally, Webster had determined that each child would receive something consistent with his or her own interests. For example, Herbert, a struggling stockbroker, was to receive the bulk of his father's stock portfolio; Gwen, a budding socialite, was to receive a diamond necklace that had belonged to Webster's own mother. Dorothy, a librarian, was to receive Webster's extensive book collection. And so on.

The birthday weekend was filled with tension. At various times during the brief stay at Webster's Florida retreat, each of the children was summoned into the study to talk about their father's plans to reconfigure his will. The study was an imposing room, with a large oak desk in the middle and three of the four walls taken up by shelves housing his remarkable collection of reference works. It could be said that

Webster's children lived in fear of their father. But tension gave way to tragedy early Sunday afternoon, when Marion Webster was found dead at his desk, the victim of a single gunshot wound to the chest.

As is so often the case, Inspector Forsooth wasn't called in until after the initial investigation had failed. One of the reasons for that failure was that none of the six children had much to say about Webster's plans for his will.

Said Biff, "Everything that Dad did or said was misinterpreted, unless you knew him awfully well. Me, I was born on April Fool's Day. Maybe I learned early that things aren't always what they seem."

What was known is that the murder occurred in the early afternoon, following lunch. Gwen had made the lunch, and Laura had prepared the dessert. After lunch, Laura, Dorothy, and Herbert were outside by the pool when they heard a shot. They rushed into the study and found nothing except their father's dead body.

The other family members then turned up in short order. But if anyone saw anything of great importance, they weren't saying so. As if this wasn't frustrating enough, no murder weapon turned up, even though the investigators searched the house very carefully.

The only real evidence was a piece of paper found on Webster's desk that seemed to shed light on his intentions with regard to his children. But the note contained only cryptic phrases:

- I have decided to "rearrange" a portion of my will.

- Bond portfolio is satisfactory—generates income.

- Plan to decrease Gwen's inheritance will be put on ice.

- Herb/pasta salad was commendable, and deserving of recognition. But a disappointment after that.

- Finally, I've decided that book donations will be limited, but funding for libraries will increase. (I'm sorry that signs got crossed.)

Inspector Forsooth, after getting used to Webster's strange method of communication, was able to solve the case and obtain a confession. He was also able to determine what happened to the murder weapon by concluding that the killer must have returned to the crime scene during a lull in the first, sloppy investigation. With that in mind, here are your questions:

1) *Who killed Marion Webster?*

2) *Where was the murder weapon hidden after the crime?*

3) *Which of the children was Webster going to treat harshly in his revised will? (One of them is the killer.)*

INSPECTOR FORSOOTH ANSWERS YOUR QUESTIONS

Q1–Why is "rearrange" in quotes?

Because "rear range" is the same thing as "back burner," meaning that some of the will was being left unchanged for now.

Q2–Does the "Herb" in Herb/pasta salad refer to Herbert?

Yes, it does.

Q3–Was Webster referring to lunch when he said "a disappointment"?

No!

Q4–Was Webster the sort of guy who would change his will over a stupid dessert?

You never know with Webster, but one has to believe that he wasn't that strange.

Q5–Is there a distinction between a stock portfolio and a bond portfolio?

There sure is. The bond portfolio was not going to Herbert the stockbroker.

Q6–Why does Webster's note say "Bond portfolio is satisfactory—generates income"?

Because the name of the person who deserves the income is right there, if you look hard enough.

Q7–What was Eugene to inherit?

I think that question was just answered!

Q8–Is it important that Biff was born on April Fool's Day?

In an incredibly obscure way, yes.

Q9–Did they have pasta salad for lunch?

There is no evidence to suggest that they did.

Q10–Was Herb's childhood commendable?

Apparently it was, and that's what Webster was

trying to communicate. As I indicated in my prior answer, whether they actually had pasta salad for lunch is anyone's guess.

Q11–Does "signs" refer to signs of the zodiac?

Yes!

Q12–How many "losers" were there in Webster's revised will?

There were three. And remember, every one of Webster's children is accounted for in his cryptic notes!

Can you solve the mystery?

Solution on pages 338–340.

8

COURTROOM MYSTERIES

THE MURDER MYSTERIES in this chapter are all unraveled in the courtroom. In each one, someone stands accused of a crime. And it is up to the jury—you—to untangle the evidence and find the defendant guilty or not guilty. Of course, as you'll discover, it's never that simple. There is always a twist. Was the murder a frame-up? Was it an accident? Was it a suicide made to look like murder? Or did something even more devious happen?

Begin by reading the court case. Consider the "Trial Witnesses & Evidence" section at the end of the story and note the minimum number of clues required to reach an informed verdict. Choose from the five possibilities which pieces of evidence you'll review first. Examine the clues one at a time and try to digest each clue before you consider the next.

Very few readers will be able to solve a case and reach a verdict with the recommended minimum number of clues. Most readers will need to see all five pieces of evidence before going into deliberation.

In the "Jury Deliberation" section, you as a member of the sitting jury, need to review the evidence and make sense of it. If your budding theory fails to address all the concerns debated in this section, return to the account of the crime and the evidence. Take your time and try to tie up all the loose ends before you finally look up the solution in the "Verdicts" section.

Hope you'll have great fun solving these classic whodunits!

Our Man in the Field

AT 9:08 P.M. a silent alarm rang at Ajax Security Co., sending an armed guard to the midtown branch of First National Bank. When he arrived on the scene, the guard discovered masked men scooping $20 bills out of the automatic-teller machines. One of the burglars physically attacked the guard, getting his mask torn off in the fight and revealing his face to the bank's video system.

Somehow, the guard managed to pull his gun and shoot, hitting his adversary squarely in the chest. The second burglar dropped the money and went to his bleeding partner's aid. He dragged his injured friend into a light-colored car hidden in the nearby alley. Both bank robbers escaped.

• • • •

About seven miles away, a pair of workmen from the water department had just finished restoring service to a rural neighborhood. "The water was off for about an hour," the technician later told the police. "We got it running at about 8:55, then stopped for a cup of coffee. We were just heading back when Mike spotted this guy in a field. It was a full moon and we could see he was dragging something through the weeds. We pulled over to see if he needed help. And then we saw the body. He was dragging this dead, bloody body. The guy was little and didn't have a gun. So Bill held him while I phoned the police. That was like 9:25."

• • • •

"We arrived at 9:31," Officer Brill explained. "The man identified himself as Wally Heath. The body had a bullet in the chest, but Mr. Heath didn't have any explanation to offer. He invited us into his house. Mr. Heath, as it happens, lives right beside the field. The house was furnished nicely, but was kind of messy. He said his wife had recently left him, run off with some traveling salesman. He seemed more preoccupied with telling us about his domestic situation than about this body. We were there for maybe ten minutes. Just before we took him in, the washing machine timer went off. We went with him to check it and saw the clothes in the washer were kind of dingy, like they'd been sitting in dirty water. We advised him not to touch them, just in case there might be evidence. Then read him his rights."

• • • •

When the case came to trial, Wallace Heath stood accused of robbery, not murder. The corpse he had been dragging through the field was identified as the late Judd Okan, a career criminal with a rap sheet in burglary and larceny. Computer-enhanced "stills" from the surveillance camera identified him as the unmasked burglar shot by the security guard.

A still of the other robber remained unhelpful. Although the masked image did resemble Wally Heath in general size and build, it also resembled hundreds of other local men.

• • • •

In court, Wally Heath's attorney seems at a loss.

DEFENSE: My client has absolutely no criminal record. He has lived in this town for eight years, held the same job for seven, and was married to the same woman for twelve. Although the Heaths were not a particularly sociable couple, Mr. Heath has been known to be a law-abiding man with the patience of a saint. He was at home the entire night in question, watching TV and doing his laundry.

True, Mr. Heath is not willing to tell us how he happened across Judd Okan or why he was dragging the body through the field behind his house. But it is not the

Defense's job to establish Wally Heath's innocence. Rather, it is the Prosecution's job to establish his guilt, something they will be unable to do.

• • • •

You and your fellow jurors are also at a loss. If Heath is so innocent, then why won't he explain his incriminating behavior?

Trial Witnesses & Evidence

This crime can be solved with two clues.

Evidence Secured in Field

OFFICER: The field covers about two acres. Bordering the field on two adjacent sides is a road that swings around. On the third side is the Heath house and on the fourth is an abandoned well with a patch of woods behind it. The tall weeds left good impressions. It was easy to spot the path of trampled weeds. It appeared that a body had been dragged from the road into the middle of the field. We found the body about midway along that path. It was face up, the feet pointing toward the road.

PROSECUTION CROSS-EXAMINATION: What makes you think the path had been made by the dragged body?

OFFICER: We found blood and fibers along the entire path. They all match those of Judd Okan.

• • • •

Prosecution Exhibit C, Autopsy Report

AUTOPSY REPORT: Cause of death was a single gunshot wound to the chest. The bullet entered the thorax cavity between the third and fourth ribs, causing a collapsed lung and piercing the septum wall between the left and right ventricles. Death occurred within five to ten minutes.

PROSECUTION: Was the bullet in Mr. Okan fired from the handgun belonging to the Ajax Security Co. guard?

DEFENSE OBJECTION: The medical examiner is not a ballistics expert.

• • • •

Evidence from Car

DEFENSE: Officer, please describe the car that was parked by the field.

OFFICER: It was a tan Toyota registered to the defendant. It was parked on the road beside the path of trodden-down weeds. The Toyota's trunk was open and inside was a shovel. No dirt was visible on the shovel or in the trunk; so, we assumed the implement had not been used recently.

PROSECUTION: Was Mr. Heath's car searched for blood, fiber, hair, dirt, etc.?

OFFICER: Yes, it was.

PROSECUTION: And the results?

OFFICER: There was no blood of any kind. No dirt or vegetation. We did find several hairs matching the defendant's and fibers matching his clothes. Also, several unidentified hairs and fibers. But we found nothing at all matching the late Mr. Okan.

• • • •

Laundry Analysis, Defense Witness
The Defense introduces a chemist who analyzed the dirty clothing in Wally Heath's washing machine.

CHEMIST: I started by comparing the dirt in the washer to soil samples from the field.

DEFENSE: And the result?

CHEMIST: No match.

DEFENSE: Were you ever able to match the dirt samples from the clothes?

CHEMIST: As a matter of fact, yes. I discovered from the county that there had been a water main break that evening. When the water was turned back on at 8:55, it ran dirty for the first several minutes. If Mr. Heath had started the wash cycle at 8:55 or soon after, he would have filled the machine with that dirty water. The samples match perfectly.

• • • •

Evidence from Defendant's House

DEFENSE: Did you examine the house for clothing?

INVESTIGATING OFFICER: Yes, and we found nothing resembling the light-colored jumpsuit worn by the masked perpetrator.

DEFENSE: Would you expect the perpetrator's clothing to have blood on it?

INVESTIGATING OFFICER: Yes, Judd Okan was bleeding heartily. The other man would certainly have gotten it on himself.

DEFENSE: And did you find any blood at all in Mr. Heath's house?

INVESTIGATING OFFICER: We did.

DEFENSE: What? You did?!

INVESTIGATING OFFICER: Yes. We ran over the entire house with phosphorescent light, designed to reveal the smallest traces of blood. We found blood residue on the floor of the laundry room and the kitchen and trailing out into the field.

The Defense appears devastated by this revelation.

Jury Deliberations

The Prosecution has established that Okan was the unmasked robber, you and other jury members agree. Okan had been killed by the guard and was being dragged across the field by the accused. The dragging, however, presents problems. You need to consider that the bloody path leads to the center of the field, well beyond the spot where Heath was caught with the body. Also, both the shovel and car were clean of the deceased's blood, clothing fibers, and hair. Heath, you conclude, must have been dragging the body to his car, and not from it.

Although the Defense may not realize it, Wally Heath's laundry helps confirm his alibi. The dirty water indicates that Wally Heath started the cycle after 8:55. Most wash cycles are 30 to 40 minutes long. Since the bank alarm went off at 9:08 and the bank was seven miles from the defendant's house, he could not have both robbed the bank and been at home to put the laundry in the washer.

The only really incriminating piece of evidence, which had shocked Heath's attorney, was the discovery of human blood in the laundry room, in the kitchen, and outside the back door.

Solution on pages 340–341.

Death and the Single Girl

PAUL GRUBER had been living in Casanova Towers for about two years and something always seemed to be going wrong. When he came home from work Tuesday evening, his new roommate was in the bathroom, mopping up a puddle of water.

"It started fifteen minutes ago," Archie explained. "I pounded on the door of the apartment upstairs. No one's home. And the doorman's not answering the intercom."

Paul looked up at the bathroom ceiling. Water was dripping between the seams of the cheap acoustic tiles. "Ginger Mint's apartment."

"Didn't she give you a key for emergencies?" Archie asked.

"Yeah. I hope nothing's wrong."

Paul and Archie walked up one flight.

Paul knocked on the door, then finally flipped through his keys, finding the one labeled Ginger.

"Inside her place it was deadly quiet," Paul later told the police. "Archie turned one way, to the bathroom. I turned the other, to the bedroom. Ginger's body was behind the bed; so it took me a little while to see it. I called out. As soon as Archie came and saw the blood, he started to heave. He was heaving so hard he popped a button on his shirt. Archie wanted to look around for it, but I said no.

"On the way out of the apartment, I heard water running. I went into the bathroom and turned off the sink taps. I know I shouldn't have touched anything, but I didn't want the flooding to get worse."

Ginger Mint had moved to town six months earlier and became involved with Todd Iona, a movie projectionist. On the day of the murder,

Ginger told a coworker that she was nervous. Her boyfriend was going to drop over that evening. She was hoping to end their tempestuous relationship once and for all and wasn't sure how he would react.

Todd Iona is sitting at the Defense table as the Prosecutor previews the case against him.

PROSECUTION: We will introduce witnesses who will testify to Mr. Iona's jealous rages. Indeed, the victim told friends they were going to be meeting that night and she was afraid. Iona arrived at Ginger's prepared for murder. It took him only a minute to do it, using a knife from the kitchen. We will show how, after brutally stabbing her to death, Iona set up the bathroom sink to overflow, knowing that this would cause the body to be discovered. And why did he want it discovered so quickly? Because at that particular moment Todd Iona had an alibi.

Mr. Iona, you see, was a projectionist in a movie theatre only a few steps from Casanova Towers. Between changing reels, he had twenty minutes, plenty of time to sneak out and run through the apartment tower's rear entrance, using the key Ms. Mint had given him just a month before. Minutes later, he was back in the privacy of his booth, where he had another full hour before his break, all the time he needed to clean up and dispose of his bloody clothing.

DEFENSE (*sarcastic*): What bloody clothing? Was any blood at all found in the project booth or on my client? No. Ms. Mint did not ask my client to her apartment that evening. Why would she? He was working. No one saw him leave the theatre or enter Casanova Towers.

And as for having access, so what? The doorman had keys to her apartment. So did her downstairs neighbor. All the Prosecution has is the hearsay of a friend who said Ms. Mint was meeting her boyfriend. Is that enough evidence to convict a man of murder? I think not.

• • • •

Trial Witnesses & Evidence

This murder can be solved with two clues.

Officer on Scene, Bedroom

OFFICER: No liftable prints, other than Ms. Mint's, were obtained from the bedroom.

PROSECUTION: Did anything in the bedroom catch your attention?

OFFICER: We discovered a white button on the rug between the body and the wall. This proved to be from Archie Gill's shirt. In addition, we found a photograph, a torn photograph. It was hidden behind a framed picture of Ms. Mint on the bureau. It showed Ms. Mint, presumably posed beside another person who had been torn out of the picture. We tried to trace it but haven't had any luck.

The partial photograph is admitted into evidence. It shows Ginger standing in the snow with a man's arm around her shoulder. In the background is a lighted Christmas tree.

Prosecution Witness, Ginger's Coworker

GINGER'S COWORKER: I met Ginger when she moved here in April, six months ago. She wasn't very talkative, but now and then she'd mention Todd and how possessive he was.

DEFENSE CROSS-EXAMINATION: Did Ms. Mint say it was Mr. Iona who was coming over that night?

GINGER'S COWORKER: No. She just said "my boyfriend." She might have said "ex-boyfriend" once. I don't remember.

DEFENSE: So, she could have been expecting someone other than Mr. Iona.

GINGER'S COWORKER: I guess. Ginger didn't talk a lot about her love life.

Officer on Scene, Bathroom

OFFICER: Prints matching the deceased's were found all over the bathroom. Prints matching the accused's were found on the counter and mirror. A different set of prints was lifted from the sink's faucet handles. These were matched with those of Paul Gruber. A wad of toilet paper had been stuffed into the sink's overflow drain, which forced the water to pour out onto the floor.

DEFENSE CROSS-EXAMINATION: If Mr. Iona had visited the deceased's apartment within the past few days, wouldn't you expect to find his prints in the bathroom?

OFFICER: Yes, I suppose so.

Prosecution Witness, Doorman

DOORMAN: Ms. Mint came in at 6:15 P.M. She said she was expecting a guest within the hour. I know Mr. Iona. She didn't mention him by name.

PROSECUTION: Did any guest arrive by the main door?

DOORMAN: No. And I was on the desk from 6:15 right up until 7:20. That's when Mr. Gruber called down and told me the police were coming.

DEFENSE CROSS-EXAMINATION: You were at the desk from 6:15 to 7:20?

DOORMAN: That's right.

DEFENSE: Mr. Gruber's roommate, Archie Gill, says he called the front desk at about 7:10 and no one answered.

DOORMAN: Well, I was there. Maybe I stepped outside in front for a smoke or something.

Prosecution Witness, Maintenance Man

PROSECUTION: Will you describe what you discovered in the garbage the morning after the murder?

MAINTENANCE MAN: Well, something was clogging the garbage chute. I went up floor by floor until I found the clog. It was between the fourth and fifth floors.

PROSECUTION: Ms. Mint lived on the fifth floor?

MAINTENANCE MAN: Right. Anyway, I found three large towels, all sopping wet. That's what was blocking the chute. On top of the towels was a pair of gloves. This particular hall chute runs right beside the murdered woman's apartment, so I knew better than to touch anything.

The black leather gloves are admitted into evidence. They're men's large, the same size worn by the accused.

• • • •

Jury Deliberations

 The first thing the jury examines is the torn photo. This Christmas photo was obviously taken before Ginger moved to town last April. You and other jury members theorize that it is a picture of Ginger and her previous boyfriend and that Ginger herself tore off the half she no longer wanted. This leads to another theory: that it was Ginger's previous boyfriend and not Todd who was scheduled to meet her on the night of the murder.

You shift focus to Paul Gruber and the discrepancies in his story. For instance, Paul initially described Ginger's apartment as "deadly quiet." Yet, as he was leaving, Paul said he could hear running water and used this excuse to turn off the bathroom faucets.

Most jury members have no idea what part the wet towels played, but the fact that they were found in the garbage with the gloves links them to the murder. Their location, stuck between Paul's floor and Ginger's, further implicates Paul. Or possibly Archie.

Going in Paul's favor is the fact that Ginger told the doorman she was expecting a guest. Since Paul and Archie lived in the building, they would not have to be admitted. And had the doorman really been on duty all evening or not? Another discrepancy.

Solution on pages 341–342.

A Family Feud

DR. PHILIP BROMLEY was overseeing the admission of his patient to Mt. Cedar Hospital.

"It's a broken tibia," he told the administrator as he showed her the X-rays. "I put Kurt McCoy in an inflatable leg cast. He can't walk on it. He'll need at least a day's rest and observation. To be honest, the fracture was a result of a fight between Mr. McCoy and his cousin. Until things cool down between the McCoys, I just think it better for Kurt to stay here."

Kurt and Emil McCoy had jointly inherited the family garment business, but their relationship soon deteriorated. The latest incident was a slugfest during which Emil swore that he would kill Kurt and then proceeded to smash his lower left leg with a baseball bat. Kurt needed someplace safe to stay while he recovered from the trauma and worked out a lawsuit against his cousin. Hence, Mt. Cedar.

Dr. Bromley wheeled Kurt into his private room and made sure the window was latched. It was 8 P.M. The hospital ordered a security guard to monitor the hall and made a note on Kurt's chart not to disturb him until morning.

At around 2 A.M. a nurse ignored that note and poked her head into room 507. She saw no trace of her patient, but did notice an open window. A deflated leg cast on the sill prompted her to peer out the window. Nothing was on the fire escape, but below it, in the deserted alley, lay the body of Kurt McCoy face down on a pile of garbage bags.

The police initially assumed that Kurt had removed his cast and was trying to maneuver his way down the fire escape when he lost his balance. But that was before they saw the bullet hole. A .38 slug had penetrated the victim's chest and proved to be the cause of death.

Emil was interviewed the next day at McCoy Fashion's office and warehouse in an industrial

section of town. Emil showed no grief at the news. "Well, at least he won't be suing me."

When asked for his whereabouts between 9 P.M. and midnight, Emil had his answer ready.

"I was here in the office. We were having trouble with our Hong Kong suppliers. I was calling them or they were calling me all night long. I picked up my car at about 1 A.M. Feel free to check with the phone company and the garbage man."

When the grand jury convenes two weeks later, it's not Emil who stands accused of killing Kurt McCoy. It's the doctor.

PROSECUTION: The Prosecution will point out the discrepancies in Dr. Bromley's story. Kurt McCoy died between 9 P.M. and midnight. According to the guard in the hall, Dr. Bromley visited Mr. McCoy at 12:30 A.M., at least half an hour after he'd been dead, and made this notation on his chart: "12:30.

Resting peacefully." And yet at that time, McCoy was already dead. The doctor has no explanation for this, except to say that the coroner must be wrong. (*The district attorney counts off on his fingers.*) The door was guarded, the window locked. The victim feared for his life and trusted only Dr. George Bromley. Only Dr. Bromley had access. And he lied about Mr. McCoy being alive at 12:30.

DEFENSE: The Prosecution has no evidence. My client had no motive. He owns no gun, nor was any gun found among his possessions. The guard, who'd been outside the room all during Dr. Bromley's 12:30 visit, heard no sound. No gunshots, no struggle. Nothing. This grand jury should never have been called.

Your job as a grand jury is not to judge the guilt or the innocence of Dr. Bromley, but to determine whether or not there is enough evidence to hold him for trial. Despite this simple directive, you cannot help looking at the larger picture. How exactly did Kurt McCoy die and who killed him?

• • • •

Trial Witnesses & Evidence

This crime can be solved with two clues.

Prosecution Witness, Officer on the Scene

PATROLMAN ENGELS: I was the first to arrive in the alley at 2:14 A.M. The body of the victim, Kurt McCoy, was face down on some garbage bags. The body was cool to the touch and totally naked except for a wristband identifying the patient and his room number. An hour or so later when the coroner allowed the body to be moved, I noticed that there was little blood on the bags, less than I'd imagine given the nature of the wound. We also found no blood in Mr. McCoy's room. Underneath the body were several broken pieces of glass, probably from a drinking glass.

Coroner's Report

The coroner reads from his report and states that the time of death was definitely between 9 P.M. and midnight.

CORONER: Death was caused by a single gunshot wound to the chest, severing the right coronary artery and causing the victim to quickly bleed to death. Other damage to the body included a severely fractured tibia (bone) in the lower left leg. The tibia (bone) was bruised but not broken.

Prosecution Witness, Telephone Technician

In an attempt to eliminate Emil McCoy, the only other principal suspect, the Prosecution calls Bruce Turner, a telephone company technician. Mr. Turner, who reviewed records from the night of the murder, states that Emil McCoy had definitely been speaking on his office instrument.

BRUCE TURNER: No cellular phones had been used to transmit or receive any of the calls. Neither had any special services, such as call forwarding, been used to mask the destination of an incoming call. The longest time elapsing between calls was approximately 20 minutes.

PROSECUTION: And with no traffic, the McCoy office and warehouse are approximately 15 minutes away from Mt. Cedar hospital.

• • • •

Defense Witness, Mrs. Barbara Conner
(Room 407)

DEFENSE: Mrs. Conner, you were a patient in the room directly below Mr. McCoy's. Did you see or hear anything the night of the murder that might be of interest to this court?

BARBARA CONNOR: I suppose. You see, I woke up late. It was a warm night and my window was open. Anyway, I reached out for some water on the nightstand. I was kind of groggy, and when I stuck out my hand I brushed my glass of water out the window. That woke me up. I got up and looked out to see if it had hit anybody.

DEFENSE: And what did you see?

BARBARA CONNOR: Well, right below my window was this alley. There were some garbage bags there. My glass landed on top of a bag and had broken into a couple of pieces. There was no body in the alley, just the bags.

DEFENSE: And when did this take place?

BARBARA CONNOR: I checked my clock just before going back to sleep. It was exactly 12:12.

The Prosecution seems eager to cross-examine the witness, but since this is only a grand jury, it does not have the opportunity.

Prosecution Witness, Nurse on Duty

The nurse who entered Kurt McCoy's room testifies that she looked out the window and discovered the body at 2 A.M. She was impressed by the fact that the victim was naked, and this led her to check around. She found Kurt McCoy's hospital clothes neatly piled on a chair. Looking into the closet of his hospital room, she found that Mr. McCoy's street clothes were missing, as were his wallet and keys. His crutches were still propped against the wall where she had last seen them.

A police witness confirms later that the victim's street clothing was never found.

PROSECUTION: Did anything unusual happen that evening, before you discovered the body?

NIGHT NURSE: Yes. I was on the second floor at about 1:30, taking a break, when I noticed a man wandering around the halls. He seemed to be checking the room numbers on the doors. Before I could call out to him he disappeared down a flight of stairs.

Jury Deliberations

A broken glass under the body lends credence to the testimony of the patient in room 407. If there had been a body in the alley at 12:12 A.M., then the glass would have been found on top of it, not underneath. The lack of blood in the room and the minimal amount in the alley supports the same conclusion. Kurt McCoy was killed elsewhere and moved after death.

Since the guard stated emphatically that no one but Dr. Bromley had entered the room, whoever else entered or left the room must have done so through the window, which had been latched from the inside.

Had Kurt really been resting comfortably at 12:30 as Dr. Bromley said? If so, then the coroner was wrong about the time of death. In addition, which leg bone had been broken? The fibula, according to the coroner's report, or the tibia, according to Dr. Bromley's X-ray? Dr. Bromley may not be the killer, but he certainly seems to be hiding something.

Other facts seem equally mysterious. Why was the body naked? Why were the victim's street clothes, wallet, and keys missing? And who was that man wandering around the second floor of the hospital around 1:30 the night of the murder?

Solution on pages 342–344.

The Lady in the Dumbwaiter

IT WAS A CHILLY EVENING in March, 1930. England's legendary tycoon Lord Dudley was hosting a dinner party at his London mansion. As midnight struck only the overnight guests remained, sipping their port and admiring the Asprey Whites, a collection of unset diamonds that had been passed down in Lady Dudley's family for generations.

"It will be a pity to sell them," Lady Dudley sighed. "But we do so need the money, at least until this stock market thing turns around."

Lord Dudley protested that conditions were not that desperate. "How many times must I tell you, dear? I don't want you to do it."

"They're mine and I'm going to. I don't know why you're being so stubborn. Why, just last

November, you were begging me to sell."

Marie Dudley was a sensible, good-natured girl, and she seconded her mother's feelings. "Don't keep them for my sake, Daddy. Enough of Gene's money survived the crash. If ever I need diamonds, I'm sure my future husband will provide."

Captain Eugene Batts held a family pedigree even more distinguished than the Dudleys'. "Within reason," the young aristocrat chortled. "Lucky for me, our Marie is not that fond of jewelry."

The fifth and final member of the group raised her voice in disbelief. "What? How can any woman not be fond of jewelry?" Katrina Burghar was Marie Dudley's best friend from school, as daring and full of life as Marie was drab and proper.

Lord Dudley stood by the window smoking his pipe. "What's that?" Suddenly he was gazing into the dark. "I saw something move. In the garden." Captain Batts joined him, and both

men stared out into the darkness. "Someone was there, I tell you."

The butler was sent out to check but reported that the garden was empty. Whatever had been out there was no longer around.

As the party broke up, Lord Dudley swept the diamonds into their velvet pouch. "I think I'll keep these in my bedroom. Better than the safe. Someone was definitely prowling around."

It was shortly after 1 A.M. when the first gunshot was heard. Lady Dudley emerged from her second-floor boudoir. Captain Batts came down from the third-floor guest bedroom and his fiancée ran up the stairs from the library. All three approached Lord Dudley's suite only to find the door locked.

A second gunshot thundered through the hall and was quickly followed by a dull thud. Mere seconds later, when Captain Batts shouldered open the door, they found Lord Dudley on the floor behind his desk—dead—a bullet hole in his head. Clutched in his right hand was a fireplace poker. Marie noticed the open window and the brisk breeze. Captain Batts noticed the open desk drawer and the revolver lying in the bottom of it. But it was Lady Dudley who noticed the empty velvet pouch.

Exactly one month later, Lord Dudley's accused killer came to trial. "Kat Burghar, the Deadly Cat Burglar," had been on every front page in Britain. You've seen her picture a hundred times. But sitting here in the defendant's box in His Majesty's court, she is even more attractive than you imagined. The Prosecution states its case.

PROSECUTION: Miss Katrina Burghar is a daring woman with a lust for precious gems. She was determined to get her hands on the Asprey diamonds and saw the dumbwaiter as the perfect means. This pulley-operated mechanism was used to lift food and plates from the basement kitchen to the dining room. It also opened on the second-floor master suite and on the guest bedroom above that. By squeezing her petite frame into this mini-elevator and pulling the ropes, Miss Burghar managed to lift herself unseen from the dining room to her victim's bedroom, where she killed her host, stole the diamonds, then retraced her route. If the family butler had not been in the dining room just as Miss Burghar emerged from the dumbwaiter, she might never have been caught.

Trial Witnesses & Evidence

This crime can be solved with 3 clues.

Defense Witness, Katrina Burghar

KATRINA BURGHAR: I did it as a lark—to see if I could really fit in and do it. If I got stuck, I figured I could always call out and either

Lord Dudley or Captain Batts would hear me. There was no way I could get into their rooms by myself. The dumbwaiter door can only be opened from the outside.

DEFENSE: Please describe your experience.

KATRINA BURGHAR: I was in the dining room. Alone. I heard an odd noise, like something falling down the chute. When I first opened the dumbwaiter, the box was on the third floor, so I had to pull it down. Then I squeezed myself in and began to pull up. I only managed to move a few feet and then . . . The first gunshot was terribly frightening. Right afterwards I heard some mumbling, like a man talking to himself. Then came the second shot and I lowered myself down. The butler was there when I came out.

PROSECUTION CROSS-EXAMINATION: Do you really expect us to believe you did this just as a lark?

KATRINA BURGHAR: It's the truth.

PROSECUTION: And what were you wearing for this rather athletic lark of yours?

KATRINA BURGHAR: Umm. I had changed into a black, sleeveless silk dress.

Prosecution Witness, Officer on the Scene

OFFICER: We assume it was the first shot that missed, since the witnesses described a heavy thud after the second. For the longest time we couldn't locate that first bullet. It was in the ceiling, clear across the room from the desk where the body was found. The desk's bottom right drawer was open about a quarter of the way. There were fresh scratches in the wood of the drawer's inside edge. These scratches match tiny slivers of wood on the sides of the revolver handle. The window was open, but there was no sign of an intruder. The door to the dumbwaiter was closed.

PROSECUTION: Can the dumbwaiter be opened from the inside?

OFFICER: No. But you can close it from the inside. The deceased could have opened it. As she left, Miss Burghar could've closed it.

PROSECUTION: Did you find Miss Burghar's prints in the room?

OFFICER: No. But we did find a pair of men's gloves beside the body. Traces of gun oil were on them.

Defense Cross-Examination, Officer on the Scene

DEFENSE: What did you find when you searched Miss Burghar's possessions?

OFFICER: Nothing. I mean we found no trace of the diamonds, either on her person or anywhere in the mansion or the garden.

DEFENSE: Did you find anything at all?

OFFICER: Yes. We found paste copies of the Asprey diamonds. Good imitations, too.

They were in the bottom of the dumbwaiter chute.

DEFENSE: What made you search the dumb-waiter chute?

OFFICER: When we questioned Miss Burghar, she mentioned hearing something go down the chute.

DEFENSE: So, if she had not mentioned that noise, you might not have examined the chute?

OFFICER: We might have, eventually.

Prosecution Exhibit A, Revolver

The Prosecution introduces the murder weapon into evidence. A Scotland Yard firearms expert describes it as an American-made revolver, known to have been part of the deceased's gun collection, which he usually kept under lock and key in a downstairs display case.

FIREARMS EXPERT: There were no prints on the revolver, but we did find several fresh scratches on the trigger. Horizontal scratches, probably made by a hard metal object.

Coroner's Evidence

CORONER: He was killed by a single gunshot. The bullet entered the right jaw at a steep upward trajectory and lodged itself in the upper left hemisphere of the cerebrum. There was no evidence of a struggle.

DEFENSE CROSS-EXAMINATION: Assuming that the first shot missed its target, wouldn't you have expected to find evidence of a struggle?

CORONER: Perhaps.

DEFENSE: Lord Dudley was in debt, yet he continued to maintain a generous life-insurance policy. Has Scotland Yard ruled out suicide?

CORONER: The evidence does not seem to support this possibility. The revolver was fired from 6 feet away and was found inside the drawer, several feet from the body. Also, at the time of his death, Lord Dudley had his gun hand occupied. He was holding a poker.

Jury Deliberations

 The fact that Katrina Burghar mentioned the sound of the fake diamonds being dropped down the chute points to her innocence. But her story about playing with the dumbwaiter just for a lark is highly suspect, given her black silk dress. A much more likely story is that she had an assignation with some-one on the second or third floor and saw the dumbwaiter as a way of secretly gaining access.

Other jurors are just as confused as you are by the details. For instance, Lord Dudley saw an intruder in the garden, and his bedroom window was open on a chilly night. Yet no trace of an intruder was found. In addition, the upward angle of the two shots would have put

Dudley and his killer in very odd positions. The multiple scratches on the drawer, gun handle, and trigger also have to be explained somehow.

But the most confusing aspect of the crime concerns the Asprey Whites. Why had someone constructed paste forgeries and then thrown those forgeries down the chute? And what about the real Asprey Whites? Whatever happened to them?

Solution on pages 344–345.

Solutions

The Sneak Thief

The contents of the suspect's pockets do not include:

1. A key to the briefcase
2. The "return" part of the excursion ticket
3. Enough cash (and no other way of paying) for buying books

Mr. Fink was arrested and charged. It was easy to find the owner of the briefcase. It turned out that he had put the case down while buying a newspaper, and in a matter of seconds it had disappeared. The sneak thief had rehearsed his story well, in case he was questioned, but he hadn't allowed for the contents of his pockets giving him away.

The Crypto Caper

The second word is obviously a day of the week, and since it's six letters long it must be Sunday, Monday, or Friday. Therefore 342 must be SUN, MON, or FRI. It can't be FRI, because 2 would then be 1, and that would make the first word of the message OI, which isn't an

English word. So 2 is N, and the day is Sunday or Monday. The message reads: "On Sunday at six get the gang together at the Juniper Tree Inn to plan our next big job."

Crypto Strikes Again

The message read: "After the Wilton Parade Jewelry Shop job, the share out will be at the Five Jolly Sailors Tavern. Tell Nutty and Al to be there."

The Holdup

The visible hinges on the stockroom door showed the Inspector that the door opened inward. The knife could not have fallen so close behind the door without being pushed away when the door was opened. So Mr. Prince was lying. He had robbed the cash drawer himself, and to divert suspicion, made up the story of the holdup. His careless placement of the knife was his downfall and led to his arrest.

Murder in the Locked Room

Pinlever, according to Mrs. Danvers, cut the rose for his buttonhole himself, so Williams was evidently lying when he said he got the thorn in his thumb cutting the rose.

Inspector Ketchum deduced that Williams shot Pinlever soon after Mrs. Danvers left to go shopping. He arranged the backfiring of the car's engine as a cover for the revolver shot. He got Pinlever to open the door, shot him, and then took the key from Pinlever's pocket, carefully positioning the chair and jacket. He removed the rose from Pinlever's buttonhole (getting a thorn in his thumb). Then he took Mrs. Danver's thread and cut off more than enough to go twice the distance from the jacket to the transom. He threaded one end through the buttonhole and drew the ends through the open transom, holding them with one hand while he closed and locked the door with the other. Standing on the hall chair, which he had already placed in position, he led the thread through the ring of the key, pulled the sag out of it, and slid the key down the lower half of the thread to the jacket. When the key was deep in the pocket, Williams let the lower thread go and carefully drew the upper thread through the buttonhole until he recovered the whole length of thread through the transom.

Williams later admitted his guilt.

Art Fake 1

The second picture is the fake.

1. The book has its title on the back cover.

2. The subject has a glove on his right hand, but the glove on the ground is also a right-hand glove.

Art Fake 2

The second picture is the fake.

The A-branding iron on the ground would brand an A, but the other would not brand a Z as the sheep is branded. The Z would be the wrong way around.

Art Fake 3

The first screen is the fake.

1. The three signatures are exactly the same and are obviously three copies of one signature. Even two signatures by the same person are rarely exactly the same.

2. When Ben added the moon, he forgot to change the direction of the shadow of the telephone pole.

Art Fake 4

The first picture is the fake.

Ben added the weathervane which, like all weathervanes, should point into the wind. Here the wind direction is opposite to that shown by the smoke coming from the chimneys.

Only Two Cars

The police cars leave the station, cross the five-road junction and go over the bridge. At the T-junction, one turns right and goes over the bridge, turning left at the end and stopping there. The other turns left, goes over the bridge, turns right into the next road and stops there.

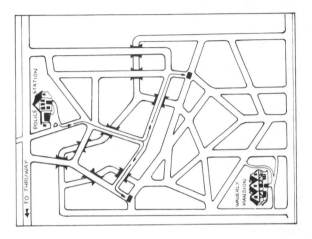

Under Surveillance
9-11-1-8-5-7-3-10-2-12-6-4

Open Windows at Scotland Yard
10 - 5 - 12 - 8 - 9 - 1 - 6 - 3 - 4 - 11 - 2 - 7

Moriarty's List

#12. (5 x 4 = 20. 20 + 4 = 24.
24 ÷ 4 = 6.
6 - 4 = 2. 2 x 4 = 8.
8 + 4 = 12)

Time of Death

1. 10:59   2. 11:54

The Secret Club

Wilson. The code numbers were devised by taking each letter of the member's surname and relating it to its place in the alphabet. A = 1, B = 2, etc. Wilson consists of the 23rd, 9th, 12th, 19th, 15th, and 14th. Added together, they make 92.

The Stolen Bracelet

Mary.

Message from Moriarty

The numbers represent the vowels: 2 = A, 3 = E, etc. Then, by breaking the message up into words, it reads: "Tomorrow I will steal the crown jewels. This will be my greatest triumph."

Witnesses to Murder
Andrew Richards, Frank Andrews, Richard Franks

Moriarty's Statement
"I'm going to be shot by a firing squad."

The Death of Foxley
20 minutes past 2.

The Dungeon
21 hours.

The Inheritance
James £1,500,000; Clive, £750,000; John, £500,000.

How Much Poison?
The wine in the smaller glass was one-sixth of the total liquid, while the wine in the larger glass was two-ninths of the total. Add these together to reveal that the wine was seven-eighteenths. Therefore, the poison content had to be eleven-eighteenths.

The Post Office Robbery
Smith shot the teller. Clark collected the cash. Drummond collected the stamps and postal orders.

The Ransom Note

Death shall take Master Sharp today.

The Missing Monet

"All three suspects had receptacles that could hold a rolled-up painting." Sherman was doing his best to make his Alabama-born accent sound British. "The messenger had a document tube, old boy. The uncle had a cane. The woman had an umbrella. And while it's tempting to accuse the last person to walk through the reception area, that wouldn't be cricket. The painting could have been cut out of its frame at any time and no one may have noticed."

Wilson snickered. "So it could be any of them."

"And it could be an employee who found someplace clever to hide the painting. But only one suspect arrived limping on one leg and departed limping on the other. I think if you examine the older gentleman's cane, you'll find that it's hollow."

"You may be right," the sergeant said. "We'll check it out. But let me fill you in on something, old boy. You're no relation to Sherlock Holmes. Sherlock Holmes was fictional."

Sherman laughed. "Nonsense. Why would Dr. Watson make up those stories if they weren't true?"

"Because Dr. Watson was also fict. . .Oh, forget it."

The Pointing Corpse

Sergeant Wilson scratched his head. "There's no way you can know what he was pointing at."

"Oh, yes, there is," Sherman said. "His battery's dead."

"So what?"

"So, a dead battery probably means his lights were on."

Sherman checked the dashboard and saw that he was right.

"Let's say Mervin had a rendezvous here last night with someone from the Charity Board, perhaps to get information for his story. That person realized Mervin was getting too close to the truth and killed him. But before dying, Mervin saw something."

"Yeah, yeah," Wilson growled. "And he pointed to it. But which of the three things was he pointing at?"

"It was night, remember? The Lake and the trees would have been invisible in the dark, especially with all the cloud cover we've had lately.

The one visible thing would have been that glowing neon sign. That's what Mervin meant. The killer was Arthur Curtis."

All in the Family

"George Gleason didn't have a chance to ask any questions," Wilson explained confidently. "He saw the victim's bloody head and the rifle and assumed Lovett had been shot. But, of course, he hadn't been."

"And that indicates his innocence?"

"Absolutely. He's protecting his kids."

"Which is exactly what he wants us to think."

Wilson frowned. "What are you talking about?"

"Gleason wants us to think he's making a false confession. He knew we'd pick up on his mistake and strike him off our suspect list. Very clever of him."

"How do you figure that?"

"Because he knew Lovett had been killed last night. Lovett is often here early, but he rarely stays past noon. An innocent man would have assumed Lovett had been killed this morning. Only the person who telephoned him last night and lured him here would know when Lovett had been ambushed and killed."

An Alarming Jewel Heist

"The alarm didn't catch anyone." Zach still sounded angry.

"Yes, it did. Tell me, Zach. How long do you think the thief took to clean you out?"

Zach glanced around the showroom.

"A minimum of five minutes, probably ten."

"And yet, when the police got here two minutes after the alarm, the burglar was already gone."

"Yeah." Zach scratched his head. "That's impossible."

"Not if the burglar was already inside. After we left, he came out of hiding and took what he wanted. He set off the alarm when he left the shop, not when he arrived."

"You say he. It was a man?"

"It was Sam Wells. He was the only person we didn't actually see exiting the shop. He must have hid in a closet or behind a counter until after we left. It had to be him. No one else could have come in while we were still here, not without setting off the door buzzer."

Trick or Treat

"The accident was staged," Sherman whispered to his friend. "Someone came in the back way, probably bringing the mask and candy, too. Miss Cleghorn was pushed down the stairs and the scene was set. You were meant to come to the exact conclusion you came to."

"Get off it," Wilson growled. "Every death isn't a murder."

"Those pearls at the top of the stairs? You try slipping on them and see if they stay in place. In a real accident, the string would break. At the very least, the pearls would have slid out from under her feet."

"Oh." Wilson took a deep breath. "I see your point."

"If I were you, I'd question Emma. We never mentioned that Miss Wilson had fallen down the stairs and yet she instantly assumed it."

Brotherly Love

Pat knew that Tom's body was found at the cottage when no one told him.

Flying Thief

She said the alarm didn't work because the electricity was off, yet the security camera was working.

Jacked Up

They didn't get the wheels, but they left the car jacked up with the jack from their trunk.

Motorcycle Mischief

Tom said he put his right leg down when he stopped, hence the bandage. Motorcycle safety classes teach you to put your left foot down first, because the brake is on the right side!

Murdered Miss

He claims to have been gone for over two hours before he even called the police, yet the ice in the glasses had not melted.

Murder Between Friends

Dr. Quicksolve suspected Tweeter. Her hearing seemed fine and her music was not loud enough to drown out the sound of gunshots. The hall was quiet and the music did not interfere with their conversation. She may have been angry with Terry for complaining about her music.

Many hearing-impaired people would be able to hear gunshots. Miss Blossom's Labrador was apparently a "hearing-ear dog," who brought her to the door when Dr. Quicksolve knocked quietly. There was no reason to suspect Miss Blossom.

Jokers Wild

Miss Forkton said she had just arrived home, yet her car was frosted over.

Threat

The driver said they were looking at a map, yet he had not turned on the interior light to read it.

Claude Viciously

Being a circus performer, Stretch would have known lion tamers use blanks, yet he said "bullets." He could only have known that there had been bullets in the gun if he was the one who took them out.

The Mings' Things

Dr. Quicksolve was not talking to Jade Greene.

He was talking to Diana, because she said, "You will get them back," when she could only have known one vase was missing by looking down the hallway at the empty end of the mantel.

Roadblock

Dr. Quicksolve suspected the driver and guard. He noticed that they seemed to have taken thirty minutes to go five miles. They left at six o'clock and called about the roadblock at six-thirty. It took Officer Longarm only five minutes to get there from the bank. They had plenty of time to stop and pull the tree across the road with partners who then tied them up so that they looked innocent.

Brake for Diamonds

Dr. Quicksolve suspected that one of the racers had robbed the bank during the excitement of the race, wearing a raincoat to cover his riding outfit, and planning to slip back into the race without being seen. Then he used the race as his cover. Because he was wearing shorts, his bare legs might have been showing under the raincoat. In fact, Dr. Quicksolve suspected the injured man of having a fanny pack full of jewels. The injured man didn't seem able to ride a bike very well. To fly over the handlebars before hitting the wall, as witnesses described, would almost surely have required the rider to hit the front brake, which supposedly was broken. An experienced rider, who belonged in the race, wouldn't have done that.

326

Tracks and a Footprint

If the killer had set one foot out of a car to dump the body, the footprint would have been outside the tire tracks. Dr. Quicksolve suspected that a motorcyclist shot his passenger, who was riding in a sidecar. To dump the body, he put his foot down on the sand between the motorcycle and sidecar or just behind the sidecar. The added weight of the body caused the deep impression. The missing clue is the second cartridge shell, which may have fallen into the sidecar.

Assault in the Mall

Dr. Quicksolve figured Kent would have mentioned any unusual characteristic to help identify his assailant. He surely would have mentioned it if the man was as tall as six feet eight inches, or if he wore a polka-dot blazer. Dr. Quicksolve thought it must be the man who was more ordinary-looking and harder to describe.

Sweepen in the Warehouse

Dr. Quicksolve didn't believe Mr. Sweepen could walk down the dark row of boxes with his flashlight on—to see his way in the dark—and with his keys jingling at his side, and surprise a man at the safe.

Either the robbers were his partners or he made up the whole story.

Robbem Blind, Attorneys at Law

If he had been sitting at his desk the past hour, he would have closed the window sooner and prevented a gentle shower from making a large puddle.

Tied Up at the Moment

Jonathon said the robber locked the door, yet a stranger walking by was able to just run into the house.

Fire Liar

Wow, indeed! This neighbor claims he slept through a gunshot, a firebombing, and at least five emergency vehicles with screaming sirens and flashing lights practically in his front yard!

There is good reason to doubt him.

If Fish Could Talk

A professional burglar would not go through the dishes, and he probably would have taken the stereo. So much damage looks like someone wanted the police to believe there had been a burglary.

Baubles

He meant the clerk was probably headed for jail. It sounds like he was lying when he said he never had a chance to pull his gun and get the drop on the thief. Dr. Quicksolve could not picture how a bandit could carry two heavy bags and turn the knob to open the door to leave, with one hand kept in his pocket.

Woof! Woof! Bang! Bang!

Sergeant Shurshot suspected Barrie Scarrie and was talking about his picture on his driver's license. Scarrie said he heard the dog bark and two shots. If a stranger had broken in, the dog would have probably reacted at once to protect his owner and their home, so the dog would have been shot first. If a friend, like Scarrie, had been let in, the dog would not have barked until he saw that his owner was hurt. Scarrie looked like a serious suspect.

B.B. Bigstuff

Bluntnose could have shot B.B. the first time he was there by using a .22 with a silencer. He could then have left and gotten rid of the .22. After returning, he could have shot his .38 twice, out the window or with blanks, and quickly replaced one of the bullets in his .38 to make it look as if he had just fired one of the shots heard by the secretary.

Death in the Garage

If McCarthy had committed suicide, he probably would have taken the pills soon before succumbing to asphyxiation. Since the pills took effect so quickly, he would have had to take them while already seated in the car.

To take several large lozenges, however, he would have needed something to wash them down with, and no beverage container was found in the car. Stanwick therefore believes that the case is one of murder made to resemble suicide.

The Case of the Dubious Drowning

Stanwick observed that there was no towel or robe by the pool. Not even a hardy swimmer would normally choose to walk 60 feet from an outside pool to the house in increasingly chilly weather dripping wet. He therefore deduced that the swimming incident had been staged, and suspected—correctly, as it turned out—Mr. Duncomb.

The Churchill Letter

The letter was dated in 1950 and refers to "Sir Winston," but Churchill was not knighted—thereby earning the use of the title "Sir"—until 1953.

A Stamp of Suspicion

A deadbolt lock had been sawed off, a door lock picked, and a sophisticated safe cracked. What then became of the saw, the lock pick, and the safe-cracking tools? No tools were left in the study, or carried in the thieves' arms, or hidden on their persons (the leotards were skintight), or taken to an escape car. If Manlich's story were true, the thieves would have had to do the work with their bare hands, which was absurd.

The Case of the Purloined Painting

Had an outsider broken the patio door glass to get in, the glass would have been on the floor inside, not out on the patio where Stanwick found it. The glass had therefore been broken from the inside.

The maid later confessed to being an accomplice in the theft, and both thief and painting were found.

The Stockbroker's Last Morning

Golding said Steinberg was seized with convulsions as soon as the coffee cup left his lips, and that no one had been in the room since his death. If this were true, the coffee cup would not have been placed back on the saucer, where Stanwick found it. Golding had actually entered Steinberg's office from his own office while Steinberg was sipping his coffee and reading the paper in the easy chair. Engaging Steinberg in conversation, Golding slipped poison from the vial into the coffee. Steinberg drank it and died. Golding then (mistakenly) replaced the cup, refolded the paper, and put it aside. Wiping his prints from the vial, he put Steinberg's prints on it and put it in the dead man's pocket. He then typed the suicide note (wearing gloves), went back into his office through the connecting door, entered the reception area, picked up the newsletter documents, and enacted his version of the tragedy.

Golding eventually confessed to murdering his mentor to advance his own career.

Death of a Kingpin

Griffith's dying message indicates that his killer was one of the "Rens." The guard was attacked at close range with little or no warning. His lack of alertness indicates that the visitors had already left, so the killer must have returned. Had the killer approached from the end of the long hardwood hallway, he would have been seen or heard first. He must therefore have used the secret passage and suddenly opened the panel and sprung out to attack the guard (and then Griffith).

Only one of the "Rens" would likely have known of the existence of the secret passage: Griffith's former personal assistant, Rennecker. Stanwick therefore deduced (correctly, as Walker's investigation found) that Rennecker was the killer.

The Bracken Park Incident

Stanwick suspected Kramer because the news vendor claimed to recognize the victim when Stanwick mentioned the Harvard sweatshirt. Miss Vaneer had also worn a jacket with a reflector, which of course would have been worn over the sweatshirt. The vendor would therefore not have known what the sweatshirt looked like unless he had been the attacker, who had to open the jacket to get to the moneybelt around her stomach.

Even if Vaneer had worn the sweatshirt on previous jogs, Kramer would by his statement have seen her only during the previous two weeks, when the seasonal chill would still have required her to wear the same layers of clothing.

The Adventure of the Negative Clue

If Orrison had just finished slicing fish all morning, he would have retained the noticeable odor of fish, especially on a warm day. While Walker was questioning him, however, the shop had only a metallic odor. The absence of a sharp fish odor was the negative clue.

Table of Death

Stanwick deduced that a man planning to take part in a suicide would not bother to fold and put away a gasoline receipt, but that a salesman expecting to live and write the expense off his income taxes would.

Barnes secretly poisoned Hunter during a cult ritual, and then prepared the "suicide" note and poisoned himself.

Halloween Horror

1) Who killed the ghost?

The murderer was the girl who was trick-or-treating in the cheerleader costume. She planted a poisoned Butterfinger bar in Mrs. MacDonald's candy bowl.

2) How could the killer feel confident that no one other than the intended victim would be killed by the poison?

First of all, the ghost was the next person heading to Mrs. MacDonald's house. Second, even if the ghost elected not to take the Butterfinger bar (which was clearly the best choice available), it was late in the evening, and it was unlikely that another trick-or-treater would come along. Finally, even if the candy bar had not been selected by the ghost or anyone else, Mrs. MacDonald wasn't going to eat it, just as she apparently didn't eat her taffy. You don't see many octogenarians with dentures sinking their (false) teeth into a chewy candy bar.

3) How did the killer's choice of costume play a role?

The cheerleader's costume was complete with a set of pom-poms. (Actually, the correct term is "pompon," but it looks like a typo!) These "pom-poms" came in handy, because they enabled the cheerleader to hide the tainted Butterfinger as she reached into the candy bowl. She then buried the bar so that it wasn't completely obvious, but so that the ghost (with sharper eyes than Mrs. MacDonald) would be able to spot it. And the rest is history.

The Prints of Lightness

1) Who killed Oscar Delahanty?

The killer was Stan Norton, with an assist (either intentional or not) from Gigi LaCroix.

First of all, Norton killed Oscar Delahanty by smothering him with a pillow. It was apparent that Delahanty must have been alive when the workmen started that morning, because his windows were closed. Ordinarily, those windows would have been open at night to give the room some air, but as we learned in the question-and-answer session, the house, being a landmark site, would not have been permitted to have central air conditioning. The need for fresh air would have been even greater than usual because of the chemicals used by the floor refinishers. The conclusion is that Delahanty was awakened by the noise of the jackhammer (a necessary part of the hydrant installation, because underground pipes would have to be exposed). He then closed the bedroom window and went back to sleep.

It follows that the killer must have arrived sometime after the workmen started, which was at 8:30 A.M. Therefore, Mitchell Quinn couldn't have been the killer, because he had been in the salon since 8:00.

Gigi LaCroix wasn't the killer, but for a different reason. She was also going to be let go by her boss, and had also harbored thoughts of killing him. Therefore, she started the fire! (Note that she expressed concern about the condition of the house upon hearing that her boss had died of asphyxia; at that point, however, the authorities hadn't mentioned anything about a fire.) Why Norton didn't arrive at the salon until after LaCroix is anyone's guess, but clearly the strangulation occurred before the fire! Note that we don't have enough information to conclude that there was a conspiracy between Norton and La Croix. In fact, their separate confessions suggest they weren't working in cahoots.

2) Who wrongly confessed to the crime?

Gigi LaCroix. She honestly believed that she had killed Delahanty by setting fire to his home. However, Delahanty was already dead by the time Gigi arrived, as suggested by his inability to react to the smoke alarm. Of course, Gigi wasn't completely off the hook. She still faced an arson rap, and was lucky to avoid prosecution for attempted murder!

3) How did the coroner's report help identify the killer?

The autopsy would have revealed that Delahanty did not have any soot in his lungs, as would have been expected had he actually died of smoke inhalation. (There would also have been any number of specific indications that he had been smothered, but ruling out smoke inhalation as the cause of death was the most important autopsy finding.)

4) What was the "evidence" that was destroyed?

As Norton left Delahanty's house, he left his footprints on the back steps, which were still not completely dry because of the humid weather. However, this entire area, footprints included, was destroyed in the fire. And that's a wrap.

The Valentine's Day Massacre

1) Who killed Rudy Marcus?

Daphne Nagelson killed Rudy Marcus.

2) Rudy's personality played a role in his demise, in two distinctly different ways. First, and most obviously, Rudy's philandering is what got him in trouble. Second, Rudy was a victim of the accountant in him. When he bought Mary Stahl a gold necklace in California, he had it shipped home, thereby avoiding the state sales tax. Unfortunately for Rudy, when his business trip was delayed, the UPS delivery person arrived with his package before he was home to receive it. The delivery person left either the package or a little slip of paper (we don't really know which) in Rudy's vestibule. Whatever was left bore the markings of a California boutique, which didn't go unnoticed by Daphne when she stopped by to drop off her

present to Rudy. At the time, she doubtless thought the present was for her, hence the smile on her face. When she got the emerald brooch instead, she may have been delighted to receive it, but she immediately knew that Rudy was a two-timer. (The fact that Rudy's trip was delayed also explains why Cornelia did not hear Mary Stahl's message. Because Rudy never called Cornelia while he was gone to tell her of his changed plans, she ended her housesitting on the 12th, not the 13th.)

3) The testimony of two particular people would prove very helpful in bringing the guilty party to justice. Which two people?

The people who would prove helpful in bringing the guilty party to justice are Mrs. Wheelock, who could confirm that Daphne had visited Rudy's home the day before the murder, and the delivery person, who could confirm that the slip of paper (or package) had been left prior to Daphne's arrival. The combination of these two testimonies would have been important in establishing Daphne's guilt.

Where There's a Will . . .

1) Who killed Marion Webster?
The killer was Gwen.

2) Where was the murder weapon hidden after the crime?

Before the murder, Gwen had hollowed out one of the thick reference books in her father's study. That's where she placed the murder weapon immediately following the killing. It didn't occur to the bungling first team of investigators to look within the study itself. (You did better, I'm sure. It's an old trick.) At some point she had a chance to go in and replace the hollow book with a real one.

3) Which of the children was Webster going to treat harshly in his revised will? (One of them is the killer!)

Marion Webster had decided to change his will to give Gwen a fake necklace ("put on ice") instead of the family heirloom. That was her motive. The others to be treated harshly by their father were Herbert (who had a fine "past as a lad," but who had disappointed his father thereafter) and Dorothy (whose library donations were going to be reduced.) Note that of the three losers in Webster's to-be-revised will, only Gwen's whereabouts were not accounted for. She alone had motive and opportunity.

The "winners" included Eugene (Gene), as tipped off by Webster saying that "Gene rates income"—meaning that he should receive the bond portfolio. The other two winners were Biff and Laura, who benefited from their father saying that "funding for 'libraries' would increase." Laura (late September) was a Libra and Biff (April 1) was an Aries. The "signs getting crossed" was a reference to the fact that the word "libraries" forces the two signs of the zodiac to share the letter "a." That's it!

Our Man in the Field

The Prosecution has not proven its case. You find Walter Heath not guilty.

Minutes after the jury foreman reads the verdict, a rookie patrolman, exploring the field behind Wally Heath's house, discovers a body in the abandoned well. It is found to be the remains of Amanda Heath, Wally's missing wife, who had been stabbed to death with a kitchen knife.

Faced with this discovery, Wally breaks down. Two weeks before he had been arrested dragging Okan's body, Wally had yet another explosive domestic quarrel, lost his temper, and killed his wife. He dumped the body into the well and invented the story about Amanda running off with a salesman. Since Amanda had no family and few friends nearby, everyone readily believed Wally's tale.

On the night of the robbery, Wally was in the laundry room when he happened to look out his window. By the light of the full moon, he could see a man drag a body into the field, dumping it only a few dozen yards from the well.

Wally went crazy with worry. The man's body was bound to be discovered. And when it was, the police would make a thorough search, finding Amanda in the process. Wally had no choice. He had to move the new body. If it were found anywhere else, the police would have no reason to scour this little field, and Amanda could rest in peace. Unfortunately, the county workers saw him in the moonlight just as he began to drag the burglar's body to his car. It was, of course, preferable to be convicted of bank robbery than of murder, so Wally said nothing to incriminate himself. In his confession, Wally described the bank robber's getaway car and the man he saw depositing the body in the field. Judd Okan's cousin is soon arrested on bank-robbery charges.

Death and the Single Girl

Since there is not enough evidence to convict, you and the jury quickly find Todd Iona not guilty.

You, however, have an interesting idea about wet towels and running water, and you report it to the district attorney. A week later, the local papers announce the arrest of Archie Gill.

Following your lead, the police discovered that Archie and Ginger had been seriously involved, and that Ginger moved to town to get away from him. A few months later, Archie followed and, unknown to Ginger, moved in directly below her. One day he approached her in the park. Ginger was frightened, but agreed to a meeting at her place. It was during this confrontation that Archie knifed his ex-sweetheart to death.

Only after Archie went downstairs to clean up did he

notice the missing button. And then he recalled Ginger pulling at his shirt. Archie knew he had to return to the scene and account for the incriminating button before the police arrived. Paul had once mentioned having a key to Ginger's apartment. Somehow Archie had to get him to open her door. He didn't call the doorman because he wasn't sure what the building protocol was. He might not have been allowed to accompany the doorman inside.

Archie removed the cheap acoustic tile from the bathroom ceiling of his and Paul's apartment and placed three sopping wet towels on top of it. When Paul came home, the towels provided a realistic impression of a bathroom leak from the apartment upstairs.

It didn't matter whether Ginger's sink was overflowing or not. The leak could just as easily have come from another source. But, finding himself alone in the bathroom, Archie turned on the faucets and blocked the overflow drain. By the time Paul and Archie finished inspecting the body and Archie had played his pop-the-button charade, the flood had developed enough to be convincing.

A Family Feud

Even though you don't believe Dr. Philip Bromley is guilty of murder, you do believe he is involved somehow, and that's sufficient reason for you to remand him to trial.

When this verdict is announced, Dr. Bromley turns

white and volunteers a confession.

Dr. Philip Bromley: I know I could lose my license, even go to jail. Anyway, Kurt McCoy came to me after his fight. He was intending to sue his cousin for assault. When I told him his leg wasn't broken, he asked me if there was any way we could fake a broken leg. He would pay me half of whatever he won. So I dusted off some old X-rays and had Kurt admitted. I had no idea he was planning anything more than a little fraud.

That night I happened to be at the hospital seeing another patient. I looked in on Kurt at 12:30 and found his room empty. I didn't know what to do, so I pretended he was still there. Raising the alarm would have simply drawn attention to the fact that he could walk.

It seemed pretty simple. Kurt was using me. Shortly after I gave the "Do not disturb" order, he must have taken off his cast, climbed out the window, and found a way to get to Emil's office, maybe a cab. He caught Emil there and tried to kill him. Emil must have turned the tables and killed Kurt instead.

Seeing the wristband, Emil deduced that Kurt must have sneaked out. After 1 A.M., when the streets were deserted, Emil drove the corpse back in his own car. By wandering the halls, he figured out where room 507 was and planted the corpse beneath the window. If Kurt had been found wearing street clothes, then people might conclude he had left the hospital willingly. So, Emil stripped the body, then broke Kurt's leg for real. Funny. Kurt worked so hard to give himself an alibi and all he wound up doing was giving his killer an alibi.

The Lady in the Dumbwaiter

You find Katrina Burghar *not guilty*.

There is only one explanation for the paste diamonds hidden in the chute and the absence of the real diamonds. The twelve of you agree on the solution but pledge never to reveal it to anyone. It would only hurt the Dudleys and destroy the upcoming marriage.

Right after the stock-market crash, when Lord Dudley was in desperate need of money, he secretly sold his wife's diamonds and had paste replicas made. Business continued to worsen, however. When his wife discovered their straits, she decided to finally make the sacrifice and sell the Asprey Whites, which she didn't realize he had already sold. The only way out for Lord Dudley, it seemed, was suicide. The right kind of suicide would preserve his family's good opinion of him, cancel his debts, and secure a substantial life insurance payoff.

Lord Dudley pretended to see an intruder. Then he disposed of the fakes in the chute and opened his bedroom window, setting the stage for his "murder" and the "burglary." He donned a pair of gloves, took the revolver from his collection, and wedged it into the outer jaw of his bottom desk drawer. Removing the gloves, he then lined up his head with the muzzle and used the poker to press back the trigger. He succeeded on his second attempt. The recoil sent the gun falling down *inside* the open drawer.

Meanwhile, Katrina was hatching her own plot. She was infatuated with her best friend's fiancée and devised the idea of using the dumbwaiter to pull herself up to Captain Batts's room, unseen by family or servants. Your jury is undecided about Batts. Was he a party to her romantic plot, or was she simply planning to surprise him with a knock on the dumbwaiter door? You'll never know.

About the Mysteries

Chapter 1 and 2: Inspector Will Ketchum and **Picture Puzzle Mysteries** have been excerpted from *The Great Book of Whodunit Puzzles* by Falcon Travis.

Chapter 3: Sherlock Holmes has been excerpted from *Baker Street Puzzles*, *Sherlock Holmes Puzzles of Deduction*, and *Baker Street Whodunits* by Tom Bullimore, illustrated by Ian Anderson.

Chapter 4: Sherman Holmes has been excerpted from *Whodunit Crime Puzzles* by Hy Conrad, illustrated by Tatjana Mai Wyss.

Chapter 5: Dr. J.L. Quicksolve has been excerpted from *Quicksolve Whodunit Puzzles*, *Baffling Whodunit Puzzles*, *Clever Quicksolve Whodunit Puzzles*, *Challenging Whodunit Puzzles*, and *Great Quicksolve Whodunit Puzzles* by Jim Sukach, illustrated by Lucy Corvino.

Chapter 6: Thomas P. Stanwick has been excerpted from *Five-Minute Whodunits*, illustrated by Lucy Corvino, and *Five-Minute Crimebusters*, illustrated by Kathleen O'Malley, both by Stan Smith.

Chapter 7: Inspector Forsooth has been excerpted from *Inspector Forsooth's Whodunits* by Derrick Niederman, illustrated by Matt LaFleur.

Chapter 8: Courtroom Mysteries has been excerpted from *Whodunit—You Decide!* by Hy Conrad, illustrated by Lucy Corvino.

Index